TITANIC

The Story of the Great White Star Line Trio: The *Olympic*, the *Titanic* and the *Britannic*

BY THOMAS E. BONSALL

GALLERY BOOKS
An Imprint of W. H. Smith Publishers Inc.
112 Madison Avenue
New York City 10016

CONTENTS

WRITTEN BY THOMAS E. BONSALL
EDITED BY EDWARD A. LEHWALD
GRAPHIC DESIGN BY JUDY CRAVEN-MADISON
GRAPHIC PRODUCTION BY HAHN GRAPHICS

THE COVER ART...is reproduced from original White Star Line literature. The front cover is from a postal card. The depiction is supposed to represent the three Olympic Class liners, all of which were to have been essentially the same. It does not show the wing bridges that were included on the Olympic and Titanic, nor does it reflect the decision, just before the Titanic went into service, to enclose part of the first class Promenade Deck. The rear cover illustrations are reproduced from an Olympic brochure issued in the 1920s. The Olympic and Titanic had essentially identical interiors.

Copyright 1987 in U.S.A. by Bookman Dan!, Inc.
Published in the United States of America by Bookman Publishing, an Imprint of Bookman Dan Inc.
P. O. Box 13492, Baltimore, MD 21203

Exclusive Distribution by Gallery Books, an Imprint of W. H. Smith Publishers Inc.
112 Madison Avenue, New York City, NY 10016

All rights reserved. No part of this publication may be reproduced, stored in a retrieval system, or transmitted, in any form, or by any means, electronic, mechanical, photocopying, recording or otherwise, without the prior permission of the publishers. Such permission, if granted, is subject to a fee, depending on the nature of the use.

ISBN 0-8317-8774-0

Printed in Hong Kong

"OCEANIC HOUSE"

NDON WEST END OFFICES.

Chapter 1. Introduction

Progress, therefore, is not an accident, but a necessity...it is a part of nature. (Herbert Spencer, 19th century British philosopher)

At 11:40 p.m. on April 14, 1912, an event transpired that changed history. Why the *Titanic*? In the first place, why did this particular ship sink? Was it design, navigation, simple bad luck--or something else? More importantly, though, why has this event exerted such a hold on the popular mind, a hold which seems scarcely dimmed by the march of decades?

There have been other ships that sank, before and since, many in circumstances broadly similar to that of the *Titanic*; the North Atlantic bergs have claimed many victims. There have been other passenger ships sunk with huge loss of life. One, a Mississippi paddle-wheeler called the *Sultana*, took an estimated 1,400 people to their fiery deaths in 1865--nearly as many people as were lost as on the *Titanic*. In fact, two shipping catastrophes--the *Sultana* and the 1914 *Empress of Ireland* collision--have resulted in more passenger deaths (as distinct from crew deaths) than the fabled *Titanic*. Still, the total loss of life in the *Titanic* disaster is the greatest ever recorded by a passenger ship in regular service. Moreover, the *Titanic* remains by far the largest liner ever sunk in regular service: The *Lusitania*, lost to a torpedo in 1915, was barely two-thirds as big. By comparison, other celebrated liner disasters--the *Morro Castle* and *Andrea Doria* come to mind--pale into insignificance. Still, the loss of life and the size of the ship alone do not satisfactorily explain the hold this disaster has over the popular mind.

The *Titanic* sinking was one of those watershed events of an era that people remember for the rest of their lives. Anyone who was around in 1941 or 1963 can tell you exactly where he or she was and what they were doing when they heard the news of the Japanese attack on Pearl Harbor or the assassination of President Kennedy. The sinking of the *Titanic* was of that magnitude. As a personal example, my own grandmother, a plain farm woman from Ohio who never in her life got any closer to an ocean liner than a picture in a newspaper, was still telling the story nearly fifty years later about that awful day in 1912 when she first heard the news. The explanation, I think, rests with the fact that the *Titanic* was more than just a ship to people and its catastrophic sinking represented much more than the 1,500 lives lost.

The *Titanic* was a symbol of an era in which material progress had assumed an almost religious status. The perfectibility of man, as exemplified by ever more fantastic improvements in virtually all fields of human endeavor (industry, science, architecture and medicine, to name a few), had become an article of faith, a basic psychological underpinning of the western culture of the time. The two huge new White Star liners, *Olympic* and *Titanic*, inspired as never before the dream of man's ability to reign supreme over nature. Then, nature rebelled. The *Titanic* struck more than an iceberg on that cold April night; it struck a body blow to the fundamental beliefs of an entire generation and prompted not only a painful reassessment of man's delicate relationship with nature, but of the very meaning of progress itself.

Having said all that, it is still difficult at a remove of three-quarters-of-a-century to appreciate the incredible impact of the sinking. After two world wars, numerous "minor" wars and a steady stream of man-made disasters and atrocities, it is hard for us today to relate to the sinking of one ship, no matter how grisly. We have become far too jaded for that. What sort of man-made disaster today could compare to the *Titanic*? The *Titanic* has been called the Concorde of its day. In a sense that is true; the *Titanic* and the Concorde both represented the outer limits of transportation technology in their respective eras. Still, it is impossible to imagine today's world being shaken to its foundations by the

Above, the White Star Line's headquarters was always in Liverpool, but its London office, Oceanic House, located in the fashionable West End of the city, was long a center of company activity.

loss of an airplane. Even the recent loss of the space shuttle *Challenger*, as painful as it was for America, hardly came close to provoking the international trauma and reassessment prompted by the *Titanic* disaster.

Throughout history, writers have produced a steady stream of morality plays in various guises all dealing with the imprudence, indeed impudence, of man in constantly trying to go places he was never--whether by fate or the deity--meant to go, trying to do things he was never meant to do. The *Titanic* became a modern morality play. Man had reached too far, gotten too arrogant and had (inevitably, of course) been brought low. Therein lies its seemingly unending fascination.

Of course, the White Star Line was not trying to teach a moral lesson to the world when it built the *Titanic*. It was trying to make money by doing that for which it had become famous: sailing liners of extraordinary size, comfort and luxury on the lucrative North Atlantic run between Great Britain and America.

The White Star Line was an outgrowth of a line of wooden sailing ships that plied the active Australian trade beginning around 1850. Thomas Ismay gained control of the company in 1867 and decided to emphasize the more advantageous North Atlantic business. The line was reorganized as the Oceanic Steam Navigation Company in 1869 and immediately set about creating a profitable niche as specialists in high class liners for the passenger trade.

In 1870, Ismay formed a partnership with William Imrie, and the controlling firm was thereafter known as Ismay, Imrie & Co. One of their first decisions was to contract with the Irish shipyard of Harland and Wolff for a new fleet of iron steamships suitable to the goals of the fledgling concern. This was to be a legendary partnership. For decades, all White Star ships were built in Belfast and Harland and Wolff built for few other lines. Moreover, Harland and Wolff, noted for their quality work, built their ships on a "cost plus" basis, guaranteeing a uniquely stable and close relationship.

The very first ship delivered in 1871, the *Oceanic*, set the standard for those that would follow. This ship was named for the parent company and carried a name that would be revived more than once throughout the

Above, the second Oceanic, completed in 1899, was the largest and most luxurious ship of her day, but was soon eclipsed by the White Star's own "Big Four," the Celtic, Cedric, Baltic and Adriatic. The Cedric, below, was completed in 1903. Each of the Big Four was, in turn, the largest ship in the world when completed.

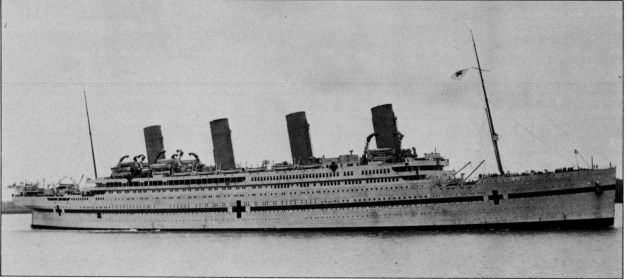

comfort never before seen on the North Atlantic. She was, however, still only a 20 knot ship capable of seven-day crossings.

In the first decade of this century, the White Star Line fell under the control of J. P. Morgan's International Mercantile Marine Company (also known as IMM). This meant that the White Star Line was no longer British-owned, a fact that caused quite a fuss in Britain. Never-the-less, Bruce Ismay, the son of the line's founder, remained as Managing Director.

Under IMM control, White Star built a succession of successful liners--fittingly nicknamed the "Big Four"-- that were each, in turn, the largest liners in the world when launched. These were the *Celtic*, *Cedric*, *Baltic* and *Adriatic*, completed between 1901 and 1907 and displacing between 21,000 and 24,500 tons each. Large as they were, though, the Big Four were rather slow; cruising speeds in the 16-17 knot range were deemed sufficient by IMM management.

The still larger, 31,000 ton Cunard liners, *Lusitania* and *Mauretania*, went into service in 1907. Unlike White Star, Cunard had built its reputation on speed and punctuality. So, the "Lucy" and "Mary" were not only bigger than the biggest White Star ships, they were also very fast. Even in her later years, the *Mauretania* was capable of sustained cruising in the 27-28 knot range and of making regular North Atlantic crossings in less than five days. This compared startlingly to the *Oceanic* and the Big Four, which were "seven day" ships at best. While the White Star Line remained uninterested in speed records, something clearly had to be done.

In 1907, Bruce Ismay met with Lord Pirrie, head of Harland and Wolff, to plan a trio of new ships that would enable White Star to regain the initiative on the North Atlantic. At 45,000 tons, the new ships would be 50% larger than anything ever built, they would be capable of cruising in the 22-23 knot range and they would contain a level of luxury utterly unknown on the high seas. The new ships were tentatively named, *Olympic*, *Titanic* and *Gigantic*. The initial goal was to have the *Olympic* and *Titanic* in service by 1910 or 1911.

The Olympic, above, and the Britannic were the first and third of the Olympic Class liners. This is an early Olympic, judging by the number of lifeboats. The Britannic was distinguishable by her half enclosed Promenade Deck and by her huge lifeboat davits capable of handling 12 boats each. Sunk during World War I, the Britannic never saw commercial service.

line's history (as popular ships were retired, their names tended to be revived). The *Oceanic* was a large ship for her day, being 420 feet in length and displacing 3,707 tons. Among the many ships that followed, the 5,000 ton *Britannic* and *Germanic*, built in 1874 and 1875 respectively, stood out for their then remarkable speed of 16 knots, enabling them to reduce the North Atlantic crossing to less than seven-and-a-half days. In 1889, the 20 knot *Teutonic* and *Majestic* appeared, rated at 9,984 tons each. That was, however, to be the last time the White Star Line tried to compete with other lines for speed. Following the *Teutonic* and *Majestic*, the company elected to concentrate exclusively on size, comfort and luxury. While their ships would be fast enough, they would never again contend for the Blue Ribband speed trophy with the other great British line, Cunard, or with the insurgent German lines.

The new direction was best exemplified by the second *Oceanic*, completed in 1899. This vessel was the first liner to surpass in length the famous *Great Eastern*. The new *Oceanic* was 685 feet in length, claimed a tonnage of 17,274 and boasted of a degree of creature

1911, with the *Gigantic* to follow in a year or two. Although the *Titanic's* two sisters have been all but forgotten, it is important to understand that the *Titanic* was conceived to serve as but one member of a team.

It was necessary to have three ships. The North Atlantic Ferry, as it was called, was just that: a ferry, i.e., transportation. If one wanted to get between Europe and America in the years before World War I, one took a ship. There was no other way to do it. So, first and foremost, the Atlantic steamship lines were selling transportation. The goal of every line was to have regularly scheduled weekly service--leaving every Wednesday, for example--between a British port (either Liverpool or Southampton) and New York and back again. In order to achieve that, a line needed fast ships and a fixed number of them, depending on their speed. The faster the ships, the fewer would be needed. Moreover, the ships had to be compatible running mates; they all had to be roughly equal in size and speed. Ismay and Pirrie calculated that White Star could do this with three evenly matched, five day ships.

As it turned out, the *Olympic* went into service in the middle of 1911, the *Titanic* in early 1912. The *Gigantic*, begun in the latter months of 1911 and renamed the *Britannic* in the wake of the *Titanic* disaster, was launched in 1914. Too late to go into service before the outbreak of World War I, she was completed as a hospital ship and sank after apparently striking a mine in the Aegean in 1916. Thus, of the three sisters, only one--the *Olympic*--ever completed a peacetime voyage.

The loss of the *Titanic* was a serious blow to the White Star Line because it upset the carefully crafted

The Titanic as she appeared while leaving Belfast on her abbreviated sea trials on April 1, 1912. The Titanic, the second of the trio, was distinguishable from the earlier Olympic chiefly by her partially enclosed Promenade Deck. This was an afterthought and the alterations were not made until the last three or four weeks before the maiden voyage. The windows confused even Captain Smith. After the collision, he instructed a group of first class passengers to board their lifeboat from the Promenade Deck, forgetting that it was not open at that point, then had to send them back up to the Boat Deck. (Harland and Wolff photo)

Following pages, the Olympic enters New York harbor on her maiden voyage in June, 1911. This is a tinted photograph, done at the time. From no angle was the Olympic more beautiful than she was full broadside.

strategy. The sinking of the *Britannic*, however, was the *coup de grace*. The loss of the two giants was one from which the line never recovered. They were simply never able to replace those two ships. In an attempt to make-do, the German liners *Bismarck* and *Columbus* were expropriated after World War I and renamed the *Majestic* and *Homeric*, respectively. The *Majestic* was acceptable, but the *Homeric* never really worked out and the line's attempts to replace her failed because of the company's increasingly fragile financial condition. A giant new 60,000 ton *Oceanic* was laid down in 1929, but only the keel was ever finished. By 1934, White Star was forced to merge with arch-rival Cunard. By the outbreak of World War II, nearly all the Harland and Wolff-built White Star liners had been sold or scrapped. It was a dismal end to a fine company.

The purpose of this book is to relate the most famous part of that company's history: the tragic tale of the *Titanic* and her two sisters. I have drawn from my own extensive archives for original photographs, brochures, drawings and so forth, to create what I trust will be a unique look at these remarkable ships.

It is my personal bias that the ocean liners of the first 20 years of the century were the most graceful and elegant ever built. Certainly there was a difference when liners grew to more than 50,000 tons. The clean, yacht-like lines of the classic Harland and Wolff designs were no longer possible due to the increasing visual mass of the superstructures and the sheer size of the ships

themselves. The 81,237 ton *Queen Mary*, for example, is impressive, but not graceful. By more-or-less common consensus in steamship circles, on the other hand, the *Olympic* and *Titanic* were among the most beautiful liners ever built. And, except for the 45,647 ton *Aquitania*, which went into service for Cunard in 1914, they were the last big liners of their genre.

Nearly all the books that cover this subject concentrate almost exclusively on the *Titanic*. This is understandable to the extent that the *Titanic* is the big name with the book-buying public. There are, however, good reasons for not stopping there.

The *Titanic* was, first of all, but one member of a trio. She was created to serve a specific purpose as part of a team. If it hadn't been for the other two, there wouldn't have been a *Titanic*. Thus, to have a really balanced account of the *Titanic*, the others cannot be ignored. More importantly, though, the careers of the other two sisters were quite interesting. The *Britannic*, the third of the trio, had an all-too-brief life almost as tragic as that of the *Titanic* herself. The first of the trio, the *Olympic*, was the lucky one. Even so, she was attacked by enemy submarines several times during World War I and was involved in at least four significant collisions at sea during a career that spanned nearly a quarter-of-a-century!

This truly was a trio of ships the likes of which the world had never seen before--and will never see again. This is their story.

Left, Thomas Andrews was Managing Director of Harland and Wolff when the Titanic was completed. He went down with the ship.

Facing page, an early deck plan for the Olympic and Titanic included this interesting sectional cutaway diagram. When the ships went into service, the Sun Deck had been renamed the Boat Deck and the Promenade Deck had become the Bridge Deck. There were eight decks, counting the Boat Deck. The upper decks were mostly reserved for first class passengers. Third class passengers found themselves consigned to the lower decks and to the less desirable parts of other decks. Second class was somewhere in between, figuratively and literally. The Britannic ended up being rather different, but the Olympic and Titanic were essentially the same. The main differences were on the Bridge Deck, where the second class promenade was eliminated on the Titanic in order to make way for a larger a la carte restaurant and 28 new first class staterooms. One of the critical design lapses of the ships is evident in the diagram: The double bottom does not extend up the sides to a point above the waterline. It was done that way to make it easier to work the boilers.

Chapter 2. Designing & Construction of Olympic & Titanic

They just builds 'er and shoves 'er in. (Harland and Wolff shipyard worker)

All Olympic Class liners--*Olympic*, *Titanic* and *Gigantic*--were to be built in the Belfast, Ireland, yards of Harland and Wolff. This was a natural decision on the part of White Star, since all the line's ships since its formation had been built there.

Harland and Wolff's story dated to the 1840s when the Victoria channel was cut at the entrance to Belfast harbor. The dredging created new land and Robert Hickson & Company, with the blessing of the Harbour Commissioners, built a shipyard and began to build iron ships in 1853. Edward J. Harland came to the firm as manager in 1854 and, in 1859, acquired control. G. W. Wolff was taken on, at first, as a silent partner in 1861. By 1862, the company had become officially known as Harland and Wolff.

Harland and Wolff was a shipbuilder in the most complete sense of the term. It built not only the hulls and superstructures of the ships, but most of the major machinery that went inside. Furthermore, it developed a special relationship with the White Star Line.

Since the very first *Oceanic* in 1870, Harland and Wolff had been engaged almost exclusively in production of ships for White Star (and for related lines controlled by the International Mercantile Marine combine after it acquired White Star at the turn of the century). Harland and Wolff operated on an unusual "cost plus" basis with its client. It built the best ships it could and billed White Star for the total cost plus an agreed upon percentage for profit. According to both shipping line and shipbuilder, this guaranteed Harland and Wolff a satisfactory profit and guaranteed White Star the very finest ships that could be built. It also fostered an unusually close, confident relationship in which Harland and Wolff could do its best work and make its honest recommendations without fear of being under cut a few per cent by a rival shipyard.

While the hazards of "cost plus" accounting are

familiar to anyone who reads about modern government procurement--those $600 hammers for the Defense Department are legendary--it must be remembered that the White Star Line was definitely a profit-making enterprise. The line was intensely interested in getting its moneysworth and the builder was fully aware of that fact. This seems to have kept the natural waywardness of "cost plus" relationships in check. Officials of Harland and Wolff were always at pains to insist that they monitored cost very carefully and, in fact, that appears to have been pretty much the case--witness IMM's decision to expand its use Harland and Wolff after acquiring White Star. Ironically, the ultimate proof of this may have been the *Titanic*. Harland and Wolff originally suggested 48 lifeboats; White Star thought 16 was sufficient. Under the terms of their arrangement, Harland and Wolff could have insisted, but didn't. As Alexander Carlisle, then Managing Director of Harland and Wolff later explained, lifeboats were expensive and there were limits to what he could, with all propriety, propose to the line.

In 1862, W. J. Pirrie had joined the company as a fifteen-year-old apprentice. By 1874, he had become a partner. Harland died in 1895, and, in 1906, the same year Wolff retired, Pirrie was elevated to the peerage. Thus it was that Lord Pirrie, Chairman of Harland and Wolff, and Bruce Ismay, Managing Director of the White Star Line, sat down to dinner one evening in 1907 at Pirrie's Belgravia townhouse in London's fashionable West End. The subject of discussion was the remarkable new Cunard liners, *Lusitania* and *Mauretania*, and the new ships Ismay had in mind to meet their threat.

The shipyard that confronted the challenge of building the three largest liners in history was a far cry from the firm that had begun in 1853. Some 14,000 workers were employed at peak periods and slips existed for the construction of no less than nine ships at one time. None of the slips, however, was large enough for the behemoths being planned. In fact, no slips anywhere in the world could take them. Therefore, three of the slips were combined to make two giant slips and towering new gantries were built to facilitate the construction. The resulting structure, the largest of its kind ever built, was called the Great Gantry.

The dimensions of the new ships were astonishing. They were to be 882.75 feet in length, 92.5 feet in beam, have a gross tonnage of 45,000. In contrast, the Cunard giants, the *Lusitania* and *Mauretania*, were some 90 feet shorter, 4 feet narrower in the beam and smaller

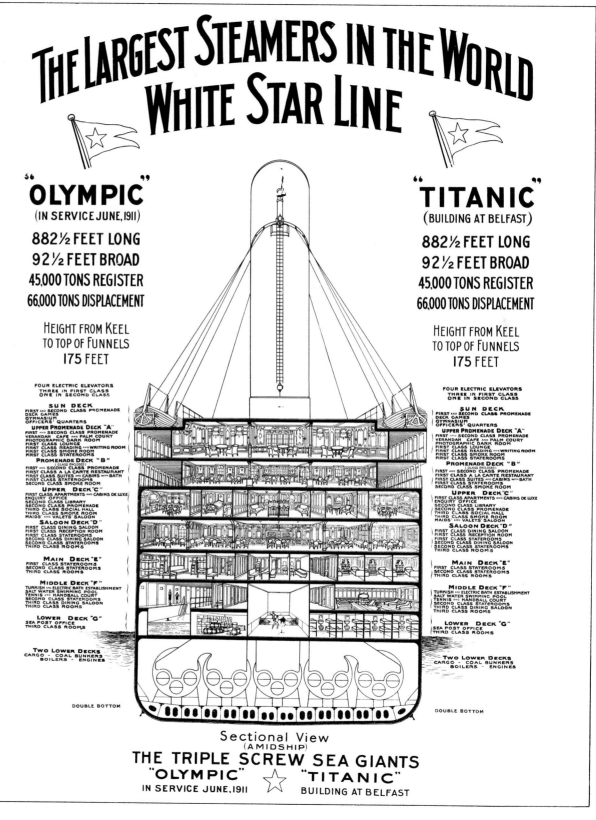

The Great Gantry, Harland & Wolff, Belfast

by over 14,000 tons.

Despite their daunting size, the Olympic Class liners were destined to be strikingly beautiful and graceful ships. They achieved this by carrying the traditional yacht-inspired ocean liner architecture to the outer limits of physical possibility. Beyond 45,000 tons, the old style just wasn't practical. For purposes of stability, ships above that tonnage required a fundamentally different--and bulkier--type of design. Even at 45,000 tons, Harland and Wolff achieved quite a feat. The 45,000 ton Cunard liner, *Aquitania*, completed in 1914, was handsome, but not of the same caliber. Harland and Wolff's secret was utter simplicity. Any designer knows that the greatest designs in any art form are often the simplest and the lines of the Olympic Class ships flowed almost unbroken from stem to stern. So cleanly and elegantly were they fashioned, one had to be right on top of them to appreciate their enormity. They just didn't look their size.

The keel of the *Olympic* was laid down on December 16, 1908. She was fully framed by November 20, 1908. The shell plating was completed by April, 1910. The ship was launched on October 20, 1910 and completed in May, 1911.

The keel of the *Titanic* was laid down on March 31, 1909. She was fully framed by April 6, 1910. The shell plating was completed by October 19, 1910, and the ship was launched on May 31, 1911.

At the time of their launchings, the *Olympic* and *Titanic* were, in turn, the largest man-made objects ever moved. Remarkably, neither was christened. Harland and Wolff did not go in for fancy ceremonies like that. Still, the launch day of the *Titanic* was a special day. This was no less true of the launching process itself.

The 772 foot sliding way in the Great Gantry had to be lubricated. This required 22 tons of tallow and soap. With this, a one-inch thick coating was laid down

The Great Gantry, above, at Harland and Wolff in Belfast was built specifically for the construction of the Olympic, Titanic and Britannic. It was the largest such facility in the world and the Olympic and Titanic were the largest ships ever built side-by-side. The Olympic was built on the left, the Titanic on the right. After the Olympic and Titanic were completed, the Britannic was laid down on the left, in the Olympic's old slip.

In the photo below, construction is underway on the Titanic's C Deck--also referred to as the Shelter Deck. (Harland and Wolff photo)

capable of enduring the three-tons-per-square-inch weight of the hull. As the launch neared, the wooden shorings under the hull were removed one-by-one until the ship was being restrained only by massive hydraulic triggers. At a signal, the simple opening of a few valves released the triggers and permitted the giant hull to slide into the harbor. There, the momentum was checked by three anchors connected by seven-inch steel hawsers to eyeplates riveted into the hull. In addition, there were two parallel drag cables similarly connected to the hull with eight-inch steel hawsers. The cables and the anchors acted as soon as the hull reached the end of the slip. In the case of the *Titanic*, the whole process took exactly 62 seconds.

A whole roster of Very Important Persons was on hand to see the *Titanic* launched, including Lord Pirrie, J. Bruce Ismay, and, perhaps most important of all, J. Pierpont Morgan. Morgan was the head of International Mercantile Marine (IMM), the trust that controlled White Star (and, in a sense, Harland and Wolff by extension). The new ship was in the water by 12:15 p.m., the launching ceremony having been witnessed by the vip's from a special reviewing stand and by an estimated 100,000 others from every conceivable vantage point in and around the harbor. Lord Pirrie then treated the vip's to lunch and a visit to the completed *Olympic*, which was moored near by. Later that day, the *Olympic* left for Liverpool and thence to Southampton to begin her maiden voyage.

The *Titanic* took much longer to fit out than had the *Olympic*, ten months as opposed to seven. This was caused by a couple of mishaps that befell the *Olympic* in the first few months of service and the consequent need for her to be returned to Belfast for repairs. In both instances, the fitting out of the *Titanic* was delayed so that the *Olympic* could be returned to service with the bare minimum delay.

For fitting out after launching, the *Olympic* and *Titanic* were in turn transferred from the gantry area to a new deep-water wharf belonging to the Harbour Commissioners. A 200 ton floating crane belonging to Harland and Wolff used in the fitting out operation was a remarkable piece of equipment in its own right. It was

Above, the Titanic, left, and the Olympic in the Great Gantry at Harland and Wolff. Below, after the Olympic has been launched, the Titanic remains under construction. In this photo, the small army of workers is on its way home. (Harland and Wolff photos)

one of the largest such cranes in the world and was capable of lifting 150 tons to a height of 149 feet at a radius of 100 feet with a list of only 4 degrees.

Everything about the new ships was on a grander, more mammoth scale than ever before seen. In each of the behemoths, there were three million rivets weighing some 240,000 lbs. Furthermore, the rivets were driven hydraulically, giving superior plating quality when compared to conventional methods. The main electrical system of the ships consisted of four 580 horsepower generators capable of producing a combined 16,000 amperes of electricity. The rudders weighed 20,250 lbs. Some 3,000-4,000 men were employed building each ship at various stages in their construction.

The *Olympic*, *Titanic* and *Gigantic* were to be composed of eight decks (nine counting the orlop deck). Below the topmost boat deck, the decks were lettered in descent: A, B, C, D, E, F and G. Below G deck were the boiler rooms, holds, etc.

The hulls were to be further subdivided into sixteen watertight compartments by means of fifteen watertight bulkheads, the bulkheads extending up through F deck. Heavy watertight doors provided communication between compartments during normal operation of the ships. These doors could be closed three ways. The captain could close them throughout the ship by means of an electric switch on the bridge. Any individual door could be closed by tripping a lever at the door which operated a friction clutch. Finally, a float mechanism located beneath the floor in each compartment was designed to rise with any incoming water and automatically trigger the doors in that compartment independent of any action by captain or crew.

The ships were designed to remain afloat with any two compartments flooded, making them capable of withstanding a broadside collision at any one of the bulkheads. That was just about the worst accident anyone could imagine in ships of this size and the new Olympic Class liners were widely regarded, even by the experts, as being practically unsinkable. The prestigious British shipping trade journal, *The Shipbuilder*, called them just that in a commemorative edition published at the time of the completion of the *Olympic*. To its credit--and contrary to popular mythology--the White Star Line never made any such claim. They may well have believed it, but they never said so--at least not for public consumption. No matter who said it, though, it was a claim destined to haunt the company for years.

The appearance of the new ships may have belied their size, but 45,000 tons still had to be moved through the water at a substantial pace. Thus, the Olympic Class liners were each to be powered three huge engines with a total shaft horsepower being projected at 46,000. Only in the horsepower department were the new Cunarders superior. Speed was, after all, the Cunard hallmark and the *Lusitania* and *Mauretania* were each powered by turbines rated at 70,000 horsepower. They were capable of cruising at 26 knots or better. The *Olympic*, *Titanic* and *Gigantic* would be content with 21 knots, not enough to set speed records but still more than competitive on the North Atlantic.

Turbines were the latest thing and Cunard was switching over to them in a big way. Cunard, however, was interested in speed. White Star was more interested in economy of operation and came up with a novel three-prop design that used two outboard reciprocating engines with a low-pressure turbine in the middle.

The reciprocating engines were of the four-cylinder, triple-expansion, direct-acting and inverted type. *The Shipbuilder* took pains to explain that they were balanced using the Yarrow, Schlick and Tweedy system

THE GREAT GANTRY, QUEEN'S ISLAND, BELFAST.

In these two photos, the Titanic is nearly ready for its launch, in May, 1911. There don't seem to be many workers about in this photo, left, taken from the harbor. In the photo at right, taken in the Great Gantry itself, there is more activity. The workers standing on the Forecastle and Shelter Decks give an idea of the immensity of the Olympic Class ships. The Titanic's name on the bow looks rather suspicious in this photo. It was probably dubbed in later.

Following pages, the launch of the Titanic. (Harland and Wolff photos)

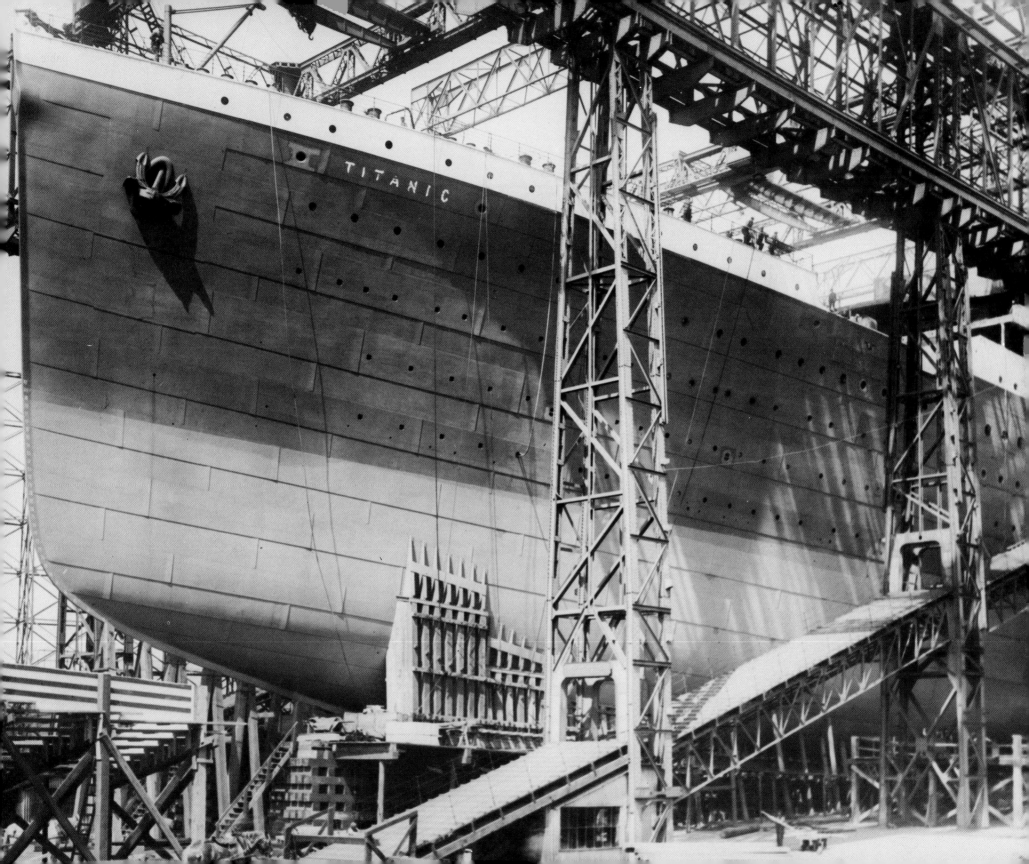

(a system whose name is so delightful it demanded mention). Each engine developed 15,000 horsepower at 75 revolutions per minute (rpm).

The low-pressure turbine in the middle was of the standard Parsons type. It developed around 16,000 horsepower at 165 rpm. The turbine was not reversible. In other words, when moving astern, only the reciprocating engines were intended to be used; the turbine would be feathered. The elegance of the design was that the center turbine would be run off the excess steam cast off by the reciprocating engines. This method had been tested on the *Laurentic*, completed in 1909, and found to be entirely satisfactory.

Steam to run all this machinery came from no less than 29 huge boilers. These were arranged five abreast in boiler rooms #1 through #5, and four abreast in boiler room #6. (The boiler rooms were numbered starting at the aft end of the ship closest to the engines; boiler room #6 was closest to the bow where the hull was beginning to taper.) In order to make it easier to work these monster boilers, the double bottom was not continued up the sides of the hull. This particular design compromise would have tragic repercussions later on.

The projected staff required to run each of these

The photo at the top of this page was taken on October 6, 1911, as the Titanic was being moored opposite the graving dock where it had been undergoing the fitting out process. The Olympic had had its collision with the Hawke and had just been returned to Harland and Wolff for repairs. This necessitated interrupting work on the Titanic. At this point, the Titanic still looked like the Olympic, the first class Promenade Deck remaining unenclosed. (Harland and Wolff photo)

The two color illustrations at right have been taken from a children's book of the period, "A Day in a Shipyard." The book is undated, but was probably published around 1911. It would be a charming book in any event, but in this case the shipyard in question was Harland and Wolff, and the ships under construction were the Olympic and Titanic! These two color prints were included among many black-and-white photos and diagrams. In the print reproduced on this page, one of the two, probably the Olympic, awaits launching in its slip. This print is misleading, however, as the ships would not have been launched with their propellers installed. That would have been too risky. They would have been installed later on.

mammoths numbered 860. This included 320 "working" the ship (operating the mechanical functions), 475 to care for the passengers and 65 to navigate. The captain and his officers were housed on the forward Boat Deck. The rest of the crew was mostly accommodated in the lower decks in the forward part of the ship.

Twenty lifeboats were fitted to each vessel, 16 of them regular wooden lifeboats and four Englehardt collapsibles. These latter had wooden bottoms and folding canvas sides, making them only marginally safe even in calm seas. One wonders why they bothered. Moreover, the collapsibles were not stored in the lifeboat davits. Indeed, two of them were lashed to the roof of the officers' quarters with absolutely no mechanism available to get them down in the event they were needed. They were clearly not meant for use in normal circumstances (but, then, what lifeboat is?).

Board of Trade regulations required ships of more than 10,000 tons to carry 16 lifeboats. This number was woefully inadequate for the number of people projected to be sailing on each of the new liners. In fact, Alexander Carlisle, Managing Director of Harland and Wolff until his retirement in 1910, had initially wanted 64 lifeboats and actually had davits capable of

handling 48 designed. Meanwhile, the Board of Trade briefly considered raising the legal minimum to 32, then backed off and let the old regulation stand. Harland and Wolff submitted a proposal for 32 lifeboats anyway, but the White Star Line elected to remain within the standing Board of Trade requirements. In that they were not alone; there was not a single large liner on the North Atlantic with anything like enough boats to handle the evacuation of all passengers and crew. To have provided a comprehensive number of boats on the Olympic Class ships would not only have cost a lot of money, it would have made the other White Star ships

In the photo above, the Titanic has again been forced to make way for a wounded Olympic. This photo was taken on March 6, 1912, when the Olympic returned to Belfast after having lost a propeller. Note that the first class Promenade on the Titanic has still not been enclosed--with the maiden voyage scarcely a month away! Thus, the only visible distinguishing characteristic of the Titanic was truly a last-minute alteration. (Harland and Wolff photo)

Below, the Olympic just after launching. This is another print from "A Day in a Shipyard."

The new White Star liners Olympic and Titanic are far and away the largest vessels ever built. The dimensions of each are—length 882 feet, beam 92 feet, depth (fro keel to boat deck) 97 feet, and tonnage 45,000. Their huge hulls, divided into thirty water-tight compartments, contain nine steel decks, and provide accommodation for 25

DRAWN BY G. F. MORRELL FROM MATERIAL

look bad, necessitating the costly upgrading of *them*. Better to leave well enough alone.

It is easy, in retrospect, to fault everyone involved for dereliction, but it is useful to keep a few facts in mind. The first fact is that nothing like the *Titanic* disaster had ever happened. Today, knowing what we know, we think of all this in terms of the *Titanic*, yet none of the people involved at the time had that compelling frame of reference.

The second fact worth bearing in mind is that technology is never completely safe. Compromises are inevitable. Moreover, dramatic expansions in technology always carry with them risks that are unknown or only dimly perceived. Atlantic liners had gone from 10,000 tons to 46,000 tons in a dozen years and even shipping experts were not fully aware of all the ramifications involved in a change of that magnitude. It was widely believed, for example, that the

new liners were simply too big and too safe to sink.

This leads into a third fact: the prevailing view of lifeboats in 1910. We tend to think of them as being there for the total evacuation of a sinking ship, with the hapless passengers left bobbing for hours or days in the middle of the ocean. In 1910, by contrast, they were regarded as having a far more limited utility. Since the experts did not believe the new ships could sink, certainly not suddenly, the lifeboats were there primarily so that people on a stricken ship could be ferried to rescue vessels sure to be waiting nearby in the always crowded North Atlantic shipping lanes. The advent of the wireless radio made this all the more credible. A big ship in trouble would be expected to remain afloat for many hours, or even days, with help promptly summoned by radio.

If the above scenario seems implausible, consider that the most celebrated recent steamship accident had

happened just that way. On January 23, 1909, the 15,400 ton White Star liner *Republic*, off Nantucket en route to New York, had collided in the early morning fog with the immigrant ship, *Florida*. Both ships were severely damaged, but, thankfully, the *Republic* had a wireless set. The *Republic's* wireless operator, Jack Binns, became an instantaneous international hero by sending the first ever radio distress message. The *Baltic* was nearby, heard the message and rescued all 1,700 people aboard both stricken ships. The *Republic* was taken in tow, but sank the following day--some 38 hours after the collision. The *Florida* managed to limp into port under her own power.

The *Republic* incident was widely cited as proof of the extraordinary level of safety at sea that had been achieved in the new century. People had faith in the modern technology and there had not yet been a *Titanic* to shake that faith.

TAR LINERS OLYMPIC and TITANIC, EACH 45,000 TONS

...sengers, besides a crew of 860. They are triple-screw boats, and their engines of 50,000 horse-power will propel them at a speed of twenty-one knots. In equipment ...o they will surpass anything afloat, as can be seen from Mr. Morrell's diagrammatic picture of their interiors. Each vessel when completed will have cost £1,500,000.

...D BY THE BUILDERS, HARLAND AND WOLFF

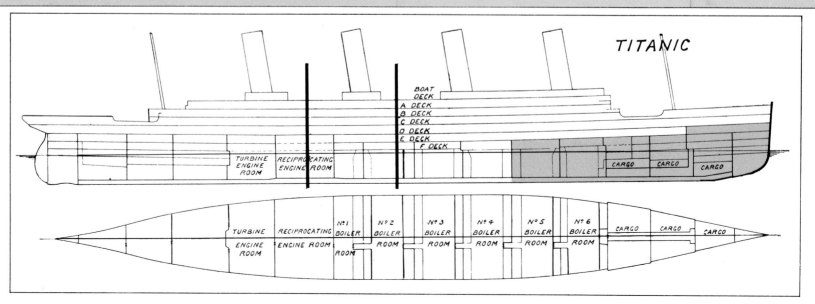

The cutaway above of the Olympic was used to promote both sisters. The drawing is generally accurate, which the descriptive text isn't, although the Bridge Deck was modified substantially on the Titanic. Note the complete absence of lifeboats on the Boat Deck! (Courtesy Robert T. Mason)

Right, a diagram of the Titanic showing the decks, holds, etc. The gray area indicates those compartments damaged by the collision. The heavy vertical lines indicate where the hull is now broken.

Chapter 3.
Floating Palaces

Going to sea is like going to prison with the chance of being drowned. (Dr. Samuel Johnson)

In the early days, ocean travel was a fearsome thing. In the first half of the 19th century, for example, it was estimated that one out of six ocean-going ships crossing the Atlantic never reached its destination. What was worse, most were listed as "missing," vanished without a trace. Many, no doubt, met dooms not unlike that of the *Titanic*, albeit on a far smaller scale. In the days before the wireless, there was no effective means of communicating a distress message, no way of leading nearby ships to the possibly storm-tossed, certainly desperate, survivors.

Furthermore, the ships themselves were small, cramped and inhospitable--very much like Dr. Johnson's prison, even for first class passengers. For third class, or steerage, passengers, the experience was immeasurably--often unspeakably--worse. It was not for nothing that immigrant ships well into the 20th century were known as "cattle boats."

For all of these reasons, the idea of taking an ocean voyage for a citizen of the 19th century was regarded with considerable concern and foreboding. Few people looked forward to the experience and the cheery Bon Voyage parties of today were unknown. The gatherings of friends and relatives were commonplace, of course, but the atmosphere was more funereal than gay--one perhaps final chance to see a friend or loved one before he or she departed into the unknown.

Naturally, the shipping companies sought to play down the risks. The comforts of their vessels, such as these existed, were emphasized. When the shift to iron hull construction came about in the mid-19th century, larger and larger ships became possible. The free market

The first class lounge on the Olympic and Titanic appears in all its Edwardian elegance in this wonderful C. R. Hoffmann photograph. This room is a minor masterpiece. The style is sort of Edwardian Louis 15th. Note the similarity in the carving of the gaming table in the foreground and the mantelpiece. Note, too, the similarity in the design of the fabric used for the chairs and the design of the carvings on the walls and posts. Every last detail was done to achieve a total effect.

being what it is, certain astute shipping lines began using the possibilities of the new technology to materially increase the comfort of their passengers. These improvements were naturally trumpeted about in ways likely to attract additional potential fares and other lines were forced to follow suit.

The improvements from the passengers' point of view between sailing in 1850 and sailing in 1900 were little short of stunning. From bunk-house style eating and sleeping arrangements (the latter often segregated) and only the most primitive sanitary conditions on a voyage that lasted weeks, the state-of-the-art transatlantic liner of 1900 was a veritable floating palace, a sort of grand hotel that moved across the Atlantic in seven or eight days. Indeed, the shipping architects sought in every imaginable way to conceal the fact that one was even on board a ship.

By the end of the century, there was a full-blown commercial war going on between the leading transatlantic lines over the quality of passenger comfort and service. Many lines concentrated their greatest attention on speed--the idea being to get the whole miserable experience over with as soon as possible. Others concentrated on the quality of their accommodations. Cunard tended toward the former strategy, White Star toward the latter. One thing was certain: No transatlantic line fought harder for business than the White Star Line, and White Star ships came to set the North Atlantic standard for comfort and luxury.

The pinnacle of White Star strategy and the blueprint for luxury liners of the future was the second *Oceanic*, completed in 1899. This new 17,000 ton ship was not only the largest steamship in the world (and the first ship to exceed in length the fabled *Great Eastern* of the mid-19th century), it reached new heights for luxury and service afloat. The staterooms, panelled in mahogany, oak and satinwood, moved a contemporary observer to write, "The lavishness of everything became surfeiting, notwithstanding that the Louis Quinze style succeeded to the Queen Anne and the Queen gave way to something 'too utter' in decadent sumptuousness. [There are] three decks of these apartments, with lavatories of costly marble, suites of baths, and every other appurtenance of physical comfort placed conveniently here and there."

As fine a ship as was the *Oceanic*, however, liners even more extraordinary were soon to follow, most notably from the major British, French and German steamship companies. The White Star Line's own "Big Four," the *Celtic, Cedric, Baltic* and *Adriatic* completed

between 1901 and 1907, were significant advancements in size and comfort. The apex of Harland and Wolff design, however, and the crowning achievement of the White Star Line, would come with the giant trio, the *Olympic, Titanic* and *Gigantic*.

The British shipping industry trade journal, *The Shipbuilder*, said upon completion of the *Olympic* that the passenger accommodation was of "unrivalled extent and magnificence...and the excellent result achieved defies improvement." At least insofar as first class passengers were involved, the statement contained a considerable degree of truth. The new Olympic class liners were certainly the finest ever built in terms of Edwardian elegance and refinement. Even for second and third class passengers, however, they represented a dramatic improvement over similar accommodations on other liners.

The *Olympic* and *Titanic* were designed to accommodate 2,435 passengers and a crew compliment of about 860 for a total of 3,295 persons on board. The passenger capacity was divided into 689 first class, 674 second class and 1,026 third class.

Of the first class quarters, *The Shipbuilder* reported:

The first-class public rooms include the dining saloon, reception room, restaurant, lounge, reading and writing room, smoking room, and the verandah cafes and palm courts. Other novel features are the gymnasium, squash racket court, Turkish and electric baths, and the swimming bath. Magnificent suites of rooms, and cabins of size and style sufficiently diverse to suit the likes and dislikes of any passenger, are provided. There is also a barber's shop, a dark room for photographers, a clothes-pressing room, a special dining room for maids and valets, a lending library, a telephone system, and a wireless telegraphy installation. Indeed, everything has been done in regard to the furniture and fittings to make the first-class accommodation more than equal to that provided in the finest hotels on shore.

Indeed. The squash court was the first ever put on a liner, as was the swimming pool. Of the two, the squash court was considered the bigger draw, judging from the amount of publicity given it by the White Star line. The "Turkish and electric baths" were saunas, more or less. They were decorated in what was described by *The Shipbuilder* as "the Arabian style of the seventeenth century. The portholes are concealed by an elaborately carved Cairo curtain, through which the light fitfully

yet put on a liner, could serve 500 passengers at a sitting. It was done in the early 17th century Jacobean style and modelled after Haddon Hall in Hatfield, England. It was a remarkable 114 feet long and ran the full 92 foot width of the ship. The reception room adjoined the dining saloon, was done in the same style and was intended as a gathering place before dining.

In addition to the dining saloon, there was a first class restaurant on the Bridge Deck (technically the B Deck) decorated in Louis 16th style. Meals in the dining saloon were included in the first class fare, but the restaurant was offered for those who wished to dine in more intimate surroundings at their own, added expense. This was the first time first class passengers had ever been able to dine alone when at sea.

The first class lounge, located on the Promenade Deck (technically the A Deck), was done in Louis 15th style with detailing being copied from the Palace of Versailles. Adjoining the lounge was a smallish reading and writing room in Georgian style. Ladies were expected to inhabit these rooms, but the preserve of the men was the smoking room, located further back on the Promenade Deck. As much effort and expense was lavished on this room as on any public room on the ship. It also was Georgian in flavor, with detailing copied from various English houses of the period. The walls were panelled in mahogany with inlaid mother-of-pearl and the room included a working fireplace over which was hung a large painting. On the *Olympic*, it was "New York Harbour," sometimes referred to as, "The Approach to the New World." On the *Titanic*, it was "Plymouth Harbour." Two little mediterranean-style palm courts were located immediately aft of the smoking room. These were furnished in wicker and had a lighter, much less formal air to them.

Even among first class passengers there was a pecking order. Some accomodations consisted of special staterooms and suites. The special staterooms, located on B and C decks amidships, were done in a bewildering variety of styles, including: Louis 14th, Louis 15th, Louis 16th, Empire, Italian Renaissance, Georgian, Regence, Queen Anne and both Modern and Old Dutch. Among the most costly of these were the parlour suites, of which there were four, each consisting of a sitting room, two bedrooms, two wardrobe rooms, a private bath and lavatory. The suites came in various configurations, but essentially consisted of two special staterooms joined by an interconnecting door.

The ordinary first class staterooms hardly classified as "roughing it," of course, even though they were

single rooms. Many were "single berth" rooms. Some were organized to be occupied by as many as three people, two in twin beds, one in an upper berth that lowered when required. Most of the first class staterooms did not have private baths, although all had at least wash basins.

First class passengers has plenty of room to exercise. In addition to a well-equipped gymnasium on the Boat Deck, there were three expansive first class promenades on the *Olympic*, one each on the Boat Deck, the Promenade Deck and the Bridge Deck. On the *Titanic*, the promenade on the Bridge Deck was eliminated in favor of increased stateroom capacity. On both ships, the main promenade on the appropriately named Promenade Deck was over 500 feet long. The smallest, on the Boat Deck, was fully 200 feet in length. One of the main features of the Olympic Class ships was their sense of space, of openness. One did not feel crowded or closed-in as one did on previous liners.

Among the many myths about the *Titanic* was the contention that she far outstripped in grandeur and elegance any other ship afloat--even the *Olympic*. In fact, they were built to essentially the same design throughout. Those few structural alterations that were made in the *Titanic* were made to refine the design based on the few months experience with the *Olympic*. The White Star Line, however, never made any distinction between them. The two giants were always advertised as a pair. Photographs of interiors in company publicity were invariably labelled, "*Olympic* and *Titanic*," with a single photo or illustration serving for both. Allowing for the inevitable minor modifications and refinements, the two ships had the same design, construction materials and furnishings. They were sisters and were the absolute epitome of Edwardian decor. All one needs to do to put the lie to the *Titanic*-was-better myth is to look at photographs of the first class rooms on board the *Olympic*. How could any other ship be more elegant, more beautifully furnished?

The modifications to the *Titanic* were limited

There were two stairways in the first class section of the ships. They were done in William and Mary style-- more or less. Both were topped by ornate skylights. The main one, also called the grand stairway, was situated toward the front between the first two funnels. First class passengers entered the ship through this stairway. It appears at the lower left. The rear stairway, located between the last two funnels, was slightly smaller and somewhat plainer, but still handsome.

reveals something of the grandeur of the mysterious East." (And that, one supposes, is how a Turkish bath differs from a sauna.) The swimming pool measured 30 feet by 14 feet. Both pool and baths were situated on F Deck; the squash court was even lower in the bowels of the ship on G Deck.

Considerable attention was lavished on the first class grand stairway, which was, after all, the center of first class life aboard ship. It extended over 60 feet from the lower landing to the glass skylight above and was impressively--if eclectically--styled in late 17th century William and Mary style with a contemporary Louis 14th balustrade. It was all surrounded with acres of oak panelling, elaborately carved in places.

The first class dining saloon on D Deck, the largest

May 28th 1927

S.S. "OLYMPIC"

= Luncheon =

Saucisson de Milan   Filet de Hareng
Fondes d'Artichauts, Vinaigrette   Sardines Francaise
Norwegian Anchovies   Smoked Saumon a l'huile
Salade a la Russe   Queen, Spanish and Olives Farci

Consomme Pates d'Italie   Potage Bonne-Femme

Broiled Whitefish, Sauce Moutarde
Fried Scallops, Remoulade

Eggs, en Cocotte, Bearnaise   Spaghetti Genovese
Navarin of Lamb, Paysanne
Braised Loin of Veal, Piquante
Fresh Spinach   Carrots, Maitre d'Hotel
Baked Plain, Boiled and Sweet Potatoes

FROM THE GRILL:—10 Minutes.
Spring Chicken, Pommes Frites

Loin Chops
BUFFET:
Gelee de Volaille

Lobster, Plain and Mayonnaise   Spiced Herrings
Sirloin, Pressed and Spiced Round of Beef
Galantine of Turkey   Oxford Brawn   Leicester Pie
Braised Wiltshire, Virginia and Truffled Ham
Ox Tongue   Roast Duckling

Compote of Prunes and Whipped Cream   Fruit Flan
Salad : Lettuce, Tomato, Beetroot and Pomme de Terre
Rice Custard Pudding
American Apple Pie   French Pastries
Ice Cream
CHEESE : Cheshire   Brie   Cheddar   Gouda
Young American   Gruyere
Fruit

First class passengers had their meals included with their fares in the first class dining saloon, above menu and above right (in a photo was taken in the mid-1930s just before the Olympic went out of service). They could, if they wanted, dine alone or with special friends on the a la carte restaurant, below. As the name implied, it cost extra but was very cozy and had its own galley. It was the first time on the North Atlantic that a first class passenger could dine alone, if he--or she-- preferred. On the Titanic, Captain Smith dined here as a guest of the Wideners the evening of the collision.

The Olympic and Titanic set a new standard for luxury on the North Atlantic Ferry, and nowhere is this fact more evident than in these color renderings. The particular renderings that appear on these two pages are from a White Star brochure issued around 1930. As such they are meant to illustrate the Olympic. The Olympic, however, was little changed since the old days when she and the Titanic first went into service, so this is pretty much what the Titanic must have been like, as well.

Upper left is a first class stateroom. This particular one is in Jacobean decor, but a bewildering variety of styles were available.

The public room, lower left, is the first class smoking room. This room was the sole preserve of the men until the 1920s, at least. The stuffed chairs were upholstered in green leather and, in general, this room had the very proper feel of an English gentleman's club to it. The painting above the mantlepiece was of New York harbor on the Olympic, sometimes referred to as "The Approach to the New World." This painting is often given as the one on the Titanic. It was not. The comparable painting on the Titanic was one of Plymouth harbor. It was in

almost exclusively to the first class accommodations. There were 28 new staterooms on the Bridge Deck (B Deck) that featured actual windows (replacing the traditional portholes). Two of these even featured their own private promenades. The first class restaurant was enlarged in response to the popularity of that facility on board the *Olympic* and a Cafe Parisien was added. This was an honest-to-gosh French sidewalk cafe, complete with French waiters. Finally, the Promenade Deck was partially enclosed to protect first class passengers from the elements during winter crossings.

On both ships, second class passengers were scattered over seven decks. Communication was either by means of a second class grand stairway traversing all seven decks or an electric elevator traversing six. The elevator constituted a major innovation for second class travel on the North Atlantic. (Of course, second class passengers still had to make do with one, while those travelling first class had no less than three.)

The second class passengers had their own dining saloon, smoking room and library.

The dining saloon was 71 feet long panelled in oak in the old English style. Passengers ate at long tables with fixed, swivel chairs. This was the norm on the North Atlantic at this time, even for first class passengers on most major liners. The individual tables and chairs used in first class were quite a special feature of the *Olympic* and *Titanic*. The second class library was decorated in the Colonial Adam style with carved sycamore panelling. The furniture was mahogany. The second class smoking room was panelled in carved oak with oak furniture. The second class staterooms were basically the same size as those in first class. They were designed to accomodate four passengers per room, however, and were decorated in a much simpler fashion.

There were two second class promenades, although the largest of these--at 145 feet--was much smaller than the smallest available to first class passengers. Furthermore, the smaller of these was lost entirely on the *Titanic* due to the adding of more first class accommodations on the Bridge Deck. First and second class dining saloons shared a common galley, which was one of the finest and most elaborate in existence, on or off the water. There were still, however, separate first and second class pantries, and the first class version was several times the size of that available to second class passengers. In additon, the first class restaurant had its own separate galley and pantry.

In general, the second class accommodations on board the *Olympic* and *Titanic* were a revelation to passengers used to ocean travel. Second class on these new behemoths was genuinely equivalent in nearly all respects to first class travel on other liners. It was second only in comparison with first class luxury on the *Olympic* and *Titanic*, which set a new standard for the North Atlantic.

Third class presented a stark contrast to the comfort and luxury available in first and second classes. Even here, though, the *Olympic* and *Titanic* were worlds removed from the traditional "cattle boat" concept of third, or steerage, class travel. Overall, the quality of accommodations rivalled that of even first class travel on major liners of 1890 vintage. There was a special third class dining saloon, as well as a lounge, called a General Room. Both were rather austerely decorated--if that is the right term--in white enamel. A smallish third class galley adjoined the dining saloon. The third class smoking room was panelled in oak, but otherwise continued the same severe simplicity of other third class public rooms. The third class staterooms, as would be expected, were mostly located in the lower decks and in the less desirable parts of the ship. There were some rooms that could take as many as ten inhabitants. Many, however, were designed to accomodate as few as two or four passengers. This was a marked improvement over the traditional bunkhouse-type sleeping arrangements--euphemistically called "open berths"--also offered on the *Olympic* and *Titanic* and the only accommodations available on most other liners. Third class passengers also had a small promenade area on the Shelter Deck (or C Deck) at the rear of the ship.

Third class passengers were not a pampered lot, of course. In this class, the White Star Line was selling transportation, not luxury. As a famous American socialite, who married into money, used to say, "I've been rich, and I've been poor. Rich is better." This was certainly true on any Atlantic liner in 1912 (and no doubt still is). As John Maxtone-Graham, one of the finest chroniclers of ocean travel, has pointed out, the cooling room attached to the *Titanic's* Turkish Bath, a facility intended for perhaps a dozen first class passengers, was larger than the galley for the third class dining saloon, a facility intended to serve the needs of more than a thousand! The White Star Line's priorities were clear. Still, if third class was only transportation, it was good, clean transportation. On the other hand, if you could afford a second class ticket, the quality of shipboard life suddenly took a quantum leap. And, if you could afford first cabin...well, they didn't call the *Olympic* and *Titanic* "floating palaces" for nothing!

this room just before the Titanic's final plunge that Thomas Andrews, head of Harland and Wolff, was seen standing alone, staring at the painting, lost in thought.

The palm court and verandah cafe is illustrated, upper right. This room was really two rooms--there being two of them on either side of the ship immediately aft of the first class smoking room--and each one carried the double moniker. They were light and airy rooms done in the mediterranean style. That meant lots of bright colors, to say nothing acres of wicker furniture. Unlike the smoking room, ladies were very definitely welcome here.

The first class stateroom, below right, is done in the Empire style. This is actually one of the parlour suites, the parlour being visible in the distance through the open door. Among the variety of decors from which a fastidious first class traveler might have chosen were: Louis 14th, 15th, and 16th, Empire, Italian Renaissance, Georgian, Queen Anne, Modern Dutch, Old Dutch and Regence. No, that last one is not a spelling error. They spelled "Regency" that way for years. (Illustrations on these two pages courtesy of Carl House)

27

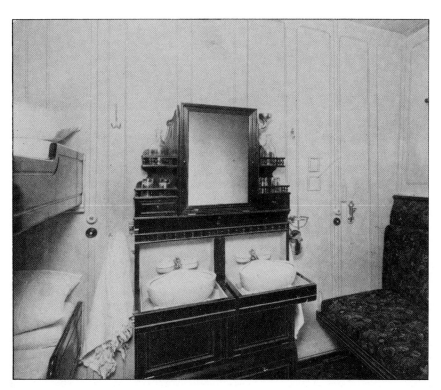

For pre-World War I liners, second class photos are generally harder to come by than those for first class. In part, this reflects the profitability of first class fares relative to second class fares for the steamship companies. First class no doubt also required some selling. Those travelling third class were of a financial status or mind-set that was unswayed by the specific accoutrements of the accommodations. This class of traveler tended to be impressed by the reputation of a shipping line or liner. Those going second cabin were of less modest means but tended to the same attitude. Second class fares would select the Olympic and Titanic because they were the greatest liners afloat, convinced the accommodations would be correspondingly satisfactory. First class travelers, however, had to be coaxed to part with the extra Dollars or Pounds, so the energies of publicists were concentrated on exploring the first class wonders of their ships. It is likely, too, that many a second or third class passage was sold by virtue of the reflected glitter of these first class advertisements. In the 1920s, as the volume of third class passengers diminished, the relative importance of second class travelers increased along with the amount of space allotted to describing the claimed splendors of second class travel.

Olympic and Titanic second class photos are especially rare. The six on these two pages are rarer still since they were used for publicity purposes by the New York office of the White Star Line, rather than by the home office. They may have depicted the Olympic, although with Olympic/Titanic publicity shots one is never really sure which ship was involved. The company used the same art and photos for both ships, so close were they in design and decor. Most were actually the of Olympic for the very logical reason that the Olympic was completed first and therefore available for photographing in a finished state for a longer period of time.

The photo, upper left, shows the second class dining saloon. One major difference between it and the first class dining saloon is the long tables and fixed swivel chairs. Separate chairs in the dining saloon was quite an innovation in 1912. Even in first class, chairs such as these in second class were the norm. It wasn't that it was unpleasant this way, but steamship architects were trying their best to make their new ships look as little like ships, and as much like grand hotels, as possible. Fixed swivel chairs just didn't cut it.

The photo, lower left, is of the so-called second class "library and ladies' room." That is, the ladies' room as opposed to the men's room--which was the smoking room, upper right, where ladies were not supposed to go. (And if they did they clearly weren't ladies.) The decor in these two public rooms is very pleasant, even luxurious, and would have passed for first class on most other North Atlantic liners in 1912.

The photo, lower middle, is the second class grand stairway located aft of the fourth funnel. It is quite a bit less grand than the first class grand stairway, but still handsome.

The photo, lower right, shows a typical second class stateroom. This stateroom was about the same size as the basic first class stateroom, but much simpler in decor. The particular cabin depicted here is a four-berth stateroom on D Deck.

Finally, the photo, upper middle, illustrates the second class promenade on the aft end of the Boat Deck. This was a scene of frenetic activity on the night of the Titanic's collision. The area in the foreground, immediately in front of the fourth funnel is where numerous survivors reported they saw the ship break in two just before the final plunge. The funnel, which was a dummy, was situated immediately above the first class smoking room.

Surpassing the Greatest Buildings and Memorials of Earth

The Largest and Finest Steamers in the World ☆ **"OLYMPIC" AND "TITANIC"**

White Star Line's New Leviathans ☆ 882½ Feet Long   92½ Feet Broad   45,000 Tons

Chapter 4.
Titanic's Lucky Sister Part I: Olympic, 1911-12

Olympic is a marvel! (Cable from Bruce Ismay upon the *Olympic's* maiden arrival in New York)

In the wake of the celebrated tragedy that befell the *Titanic*, it is not surprising that the public's attention should have focused on her, the second of the great Olympic Class liners. This development does, however, represent a dramatic about-face from the situation that existed before the *Titanic* met her doom. The *Titanic* was but one of three projected ships. The *Olympic* was the first--hence the designation of the three as "Olympic Class" ships--and it was the *Olympic* that garnered the lion's share of the fame and publicity prior to April 15, 1912. It has been noted by some *Titanic* writers that the *Titanic* went almost unnoticed until she sank. That is perhaps a bit of an exaggeration--but only a bit.

While still on the stocks, the *Olympic's* hull was painted white to show off her size and proportions. Moreover, her name was proudly embalzoned on her hull for all to see. By contrast, the *Titanic* was painted black and her name did not appear anywhere on her.

Prior to leaving for her sea trials from Belfast, the *Olympic* was opened to visitors on May 2, 1911, thousands of whom paid 5 shillings a piece to see the new wonder ship. The proceeds were donated to hospitals in Belfast. On May 29th, the extensive trials began and lasted two full days. In them, the *Olympic*

The Olympic and Titanic were the industrial wonders of the world in 1911 and 1912. The White Star Line missed few opportunities to advertise their new behemoths and it was probably inevitable that a comparison, such as the one appearing on the facing page, would be done. The structures are, left to right, the Bunker Hill Monument, City Hall in Philadelphia, the Washington Monument, the Metropolitan Tower in New York, the Woolworth Building in New York, the Olympic, the Cologne Cathedral, the Great Pyramid at Gizeh and St. Peter's in Rome.

The illustration, right, is taken from a popular postcard issued in both Olympic and Titanic versions.

WHITE STAR LINE

was tested for speed and maneuverability. The design speed of 21 knots was exceeded by nearly a knot and in all other respects the new ship performed admirably.

Even at the *Titanic's* launch on May 31st, the *Olympic* overshadowed her younger sister. Guests invited to witness the launching of the *Titanic* ended up touring the completed *Olympic*. As if that were not enough of a slight, the completed *Titanic* was never given full sea trials. It was assumed, apparently, that the *Titanic* would perform as had her sister.

The *Olympic* arrived in Liverpool on June 1st and was again thrown open to the public. That evening, she left for Southampton, was visited by thousands more, and departed on her maiden voyage to New York via Cherbourg on June 14th. Due to trouble with the coal handlers in Southampton, five of her boilers remained unlit. Still, she averaged 21.17 knots on the outward passage and an impressive 22.32 knots on the return.

At New York, Pier 59 had been extended 90 feet further out into the Hudson River in order to accommodate the new class of liners. A small incident marred the maiden arrival. As no less than 12 tugboats were puffing away trying to ease the behemoth to her pier, the *Olympic* let loose with a sudden reverse burst of her starboard propeller. One of the tugs, the *O. L. Hallenbeck*, was sucked against the ship and severely damaged. The liner emerged more-or-less unscathed.

The next three voyages were uneventful, but disaster struck on the outward bound leg of the fifth. On the morning of September 20, 1911, the *Olympic* departed Southampton with E. J. Smith (who would later command the *Titanic*) as master. Shortly after noon, the *Olympic* was rounding the Bramble Bank at the normal harbor speed of 19 knots when she encountered the 7,350 ton British cruiser *Hawke*. Both ships turned so as to proceed down the Spithead channel, and, in fact, did so on parallel courses for some distance, variously stated to have been 100 to 300 yards apart. Suddenly, the *Hawke* veered towards the larger ship. A collision was unavoidable and the bow of the

On her fifth voyage, the Olympic had a freakish collision with the British warship, Hawke. The two ships were on parallel courses in the Spithead channel when the Hawke suddenly veered into the side of the liner. Admiralty tests proved that the great disparity in size between the vessels caused suction to be created that, in effect, dragged the smaller ship into the side of the larger one. The White Star Line protested all the way to the House of Lords, but lost. The photos on

cruiser slammed into the starboard side of the *Olympic* about 80 feet from the stern. The bow of the *Hawke* was badly smashed and two gashes were left in the side of the *Olympic*, one above and one below the waterline. Remarkably, no loss of life resulted. The *Olympic* put many of her passengers off by tender at Cowes, then returned to Southampton. The *Hawke* made it to Portsmouth under her own power and was then laid up.

The common wisdom was that the cruiser was at fault. The Admiralty put on a strong defense, however, claiming that tests with models demonstrated that the vast difference in displacement of the two ships, and the increasing speed of the *Olympic* as she moved down the channel, had created an irresistible suction that, in effect, dragged the *Hawke* into the liner. The Court of Inquiry ruled for the Admiralty, although the line and Captain Smith were held blameless because the *Olympic* was under the command of the harbor pilot at the time. The case was eventually appealed all the way to the House of Lords, which upheld the lower court.

The *Olympic* was returned to Belfast so that Harland and Wolff could effect repairs. Once again, the *Titanic* was upstaged as work on her was suspended so that the *Olympic* could be returned to service as soon as possible. The repair work took six weeks.

In February, 1912, the *Olympic* dropped a propeller blade and was, again, returned to Belfast for repairs. Reportedly, the new blade was cannibalized from the poor *Titanic* so that, yet again, her sister could be returned without unnecessary delay. The fitting out of the *Titanic* took three months longer than that of the *Olympic* and a large part of the reason were the delays caused by the periodic problems that befell her sister.

The *Titanic*, which had been originally scheduled to enter service in February, 1912, did not make it in service until April. On the night of April 14th, the *Olympic* was steaming eastward from New York. The *Titanic* was headed in the opposite direction on the first leg of her oft-delayed maiden voyage--a voyage she was destined never to complete.

these pages show the extent of the damage to both ships. The bow of the Hawke was badly smashed and the hull of the Olympic was pierced in two places, both above and below the waterline. Remarkably, there were no casualties on either ship and both were able to make it to port under their own power. The Olympic was returned to Harland and Wolff for repairs. While these were being carried out, fitting out work was suspended on her younger sister, the Titanic.

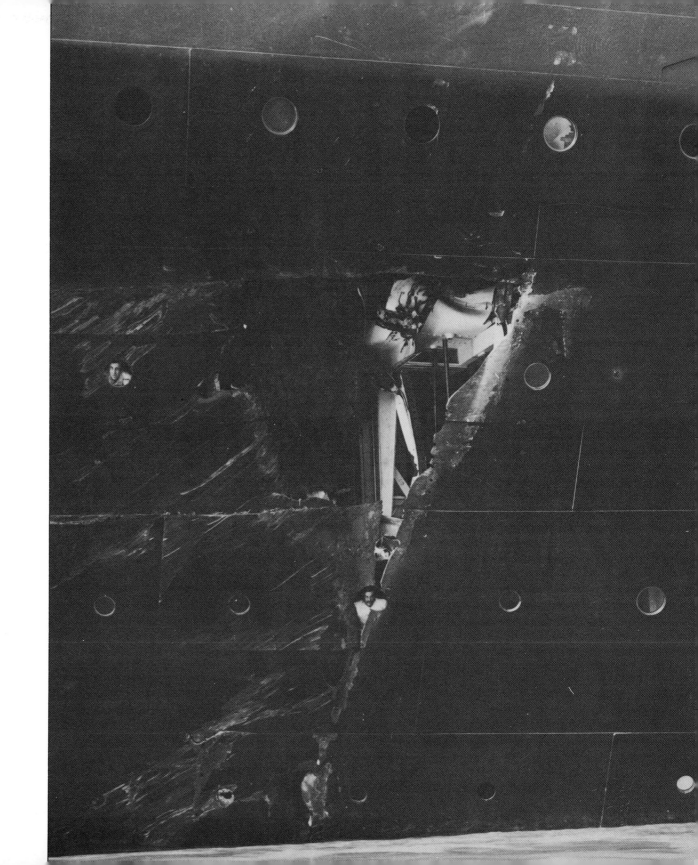

Chapter 5.
Maiden Voyage
of the Titanic

S.S. TITANIC.

When anyone asks me how I can best describe my experiences of nearly 40 years at sea, I merely say "uneventful." I have never been in an accident of any sort worth speaking about. I never saw a wreck and have never been wrecked, nor was I ever in any predicament that threatened to end in disaster of any sort. (Captain Edward J. Smith, in an interview in 1907)

After numerous delays, the *Titanic* was finally scheduled for departure on its maiden voyage on April 10, 1912, with the White Star Line's most honored master, Captain E. J. Smith, in command. The building of the new ship had been twice delayed by problems with her sister ship, the *Olympic*, which had gone gone to sea the previous June. In September, the *Olympic* had collided with the British cruiser, *H.M.S. Hawke*, and then been returned to Belfast for repairs. In February, the *Olympic* had lost a propeller. In both cases, work on the *Titanic* was slowed or suspended so that the *Olympic* could be returned to service as soon as possible. Now, with the maiden voyage imminent, a new problem arose.

Britain was in the grips of another of its periodic coal strikes. The shortage offered a daunting challenge to any transatlantic liner, all of which were prodigious users of coal, but especially to behemoths such as the *Olympic* and *Titanic* which burned the stuff at the rate of more than 600 tons a day. In fact, in order to scavenge enough of the suddenly precious fuel, other ships under IMM control, the *Oceanic* and *Adriatic* to name but two, were laid up and coal was transferred from them to enable the *Titanic* to depart on schedule with full bunkers. Qualified officers and crew were in short supply, as well, and the required compliment was hastily assembled by raiding the *Olympic*, the *Oceanic* and other ships. Only those few transferred from the *Olympic* had any familiarity with a ship of the *Titanic's* description, and none with the *Titanic* specifically. A maiden voyage is always a bit chaotic as passengers and crew both get to know the new ship together, but this voyage was destined to be more disorganized than most.

It was almost noon on April 10th when the *Titanic*

began to ease away from the White Star pier at Southampton and depart land for the last time. Disaster nearly struck almost immediately. As the *Titanic* moved majestically through the harbor at a speed of about 6 knots, the steamer *New York* suddenly snapped her moorings and swung menacingly toward the port side. It seemed as if the *Olympic's* collision with the *Hawke* was about the be repeated. While tug boats frantically attempted to get a line on the wayward American liner, Captain Smith of the *Titanic* first cut his engines, then deftly used the wash from his port engine to halt the swing of the other ship. Even so, the *New York* was dragged sideways for some distance through the channel, nearly colliding with the *Oceanic* before tugs could halt her momentum and return her to safe moorings.

Later the same day, the *Titanic* dropped anchor off Cherbourg, France, to embark additional passengers. Queenstown (now Cobh), Ireland, was reached around noon the following day where still more passengers boarded, then the new liner made for the open sea and for New York. On board were a total of 2,227 souls, consisting of 1,320 passengers and 907 crew.

The *Titanic's* passenger list included the usual mix of the ordinary and the famous. Several members of the American social register were on board, include names like Astor, Widener and Thayer. Major Archibald Butt (the Alexander Haig of his day), the trusted friend and advisor to President Taft, was present, returning from an official mission to Europe. Denver socialite, Mrs. J. J. Brown, later celebrated as the "Unsinkable Molly Brown," was there, too--in point of fact, the *Titanic* was how she got the nickname. Artist Frank Millet was on board, as was W. T. Stead, the noted editor, Jacques Futrelle, a noted writer, and theatrical producer, Henry B. Harris. Philanthropist Isidor Strauss was there with his wife Ida. So, too, was industrialist Benjamin Guggenheim. Sir Cosmo and Lady Duff Gordon headed the list of British society. This group brought with it a small army of personal servants, valets and functionaries--no less than 31 of them.

Many of the big wigs associated with the *Titanic*

The photo of the Titanic, left, was taken on Good Friday, April 12, 1912, while the ship was tied up in Southampton awaiting departure on her maiden voyage. She was dressed with multi-colored flags for the occasion and for the enjoyment of the citizens of Southampton. This was the only time the Titanic ever dressed ship. (Notice the other White Star liner being dwarfed at the left of the picture.)

were present for the maiden trip. J. P. Morgan, who controlled IMM, the parent company of White Star, had been forced to cancel out due to illness, but J. Bruce Ismay, Managing Director of the line, was there. So, too, was Thomas Andrews who ran Harland and Wolff for Lord Pirrie and had overseen the building of the ship. Captain Smith himself was something of a celebrity. He was the Commodore of the White Star Line and had been in command of the *Olympic* since she went to sea the year before. At 59, he was due to retire but had accepted the honor of commanding the *Titanic* on her maiden voyage as a farewell gift from the company. It was supposed to be his last command.

Captain Smith had done an odd thing en route from Cherbourg to Queenstown. Without explanation, he had, for a time, sent the ship through some "S"-type turning maneuvers. It seemed as if the master was trying to get the mettle of his new command. Considering the grossly abbreviated sea trials given the *Titanic*, perhaps Captain Smith thought an *ad hoc* version was appropriate before open sea was reached.

In any case, the westward voyage from Queenstown was uneventful for the first several days. Captain Smith gradually increased his speed from day to day, gently breaking in the new engines. On the first day out, 386 miles were covered. On the second day, the figure rose to 519 miles and, on the third, to 546 miles. Later that same day, Sunday the 14th of April, Captain Smith told some of the passengers that he intended to open her up a bit more the following day, as well.

The only sour note on the voyage--and one of which the passengers were kept blissfully unaware--was that the ship was on fire! For days there had been a smoldering inferno in one of the coal bunkers. Coal was tricky to handle and incidents of that nature were, unfortunately, not unusual in coal-burning ships. The dust was a constant annoyance; it got into everything, clogging machinery and anything else in range, and was flammable besides. The coal itself had to be kept at a proper level of humidity or it was subject to spontaneous combustion. This latter danger was, in

Steamship companies provided stationery, usually featuring the line's emblem or an image of the ship. With the Olympic and Titanic there were may have been three, perhaps four, different postcards offered for the use of those on board. One appears on the front cover of this book. Another appears above. Some of these cards are known to have been mailed from the Titanic during her stop at Queenstown. (Courtesy Gary R. Spence)

fact, what had happened while the ship was still tied up at Southampton and crew members had been fighting the fire around the clock ever since. Late on Sunday, Captain Smith received the encouraging news that the fire was finally under control. The last thing he had wanted was to mar the maiden voyage of his final command by having to call in the fire authorities when the ship docked at the White Star Pier in New York.

That Sunday had begun auspiciously enough with Captain Smith leading Divine Services for the passengers. Later on, however, the radio traffic monitored by the Marconi wireless room aft of the bridge began to tell of sightings of ice in the waters a few hours ahead. The *Titanic's* wireless operators even relayed one of these messages to other ships. In all, six warnings had been sent to the bridge, one of which had been given to the captain himself at midday. The captain, in turn, had given it to Bruce Ismay. That evening, Captain Smith retrieved the message from Ismay explaining that he wanted to post it on the bridge. Still, the ship steamed on as Captain Smith dined in the a la carte restaurant, a dinner guest of the

Wideners. Around 9 o'clock, the captain excused himself to check in with the bridge, then retired to his cabin.

At 10 o'clock that evening, the watch on the bridge changed. The new watch crew was headed by First Officer Murdoch, who had served with Captain Smith on board the *Olympic*.

Around 11 o'clock, the Marconi wireless operator of the *Titanic*, Jack Phillips, received a message--yet another ice warning--this time coming from an ice-bound ship nearby named the *Californian*. The operator on the 6,223 ton Leyland liner, Cyril Evans, was rudely cut off, however, before he could finish it. "Shut up, shut up," Phillips interjected, "I'm busy. I'm working [the wireless station at] Cape Race." Evans did more than shut up; he turned off his radio set and went to bed.

At 11:40 the cry came from the crow's nest, "Iceberg right ahead!"

Murdoch instantaneously took evasive action. He ordered the ship's engines stopped, then called for full speed astern. At the same time, he ordered a hard turn to port. For what seemed an eternity, the ship bore inexorably down on the iceberg. It took perhaps half-a-

Above, some of the officers and crew of the Titanic. The master of the ship was Edward J. Smith, appearing at the center with his dog. The others, going clockwise from Smith's left, are: Herbert W. McElroy, the Chief Purser; Henry T. Wilde, the Chief Officer; Herbert J. Pitman, the Third Officer; Harold Bride, the junior wireless operator; Harold G. Lowe, the Fifth Officer; Jack Phillips, the senior wireless operator; and William M. Murdoch, the First Officer. Of this group, only Pitman, Bride and Lowe survived. Murdoch, on the bridge when the collision occurred, may have committed suicide just before the ship went down. Phillips and Bride, swimming in the water after the sinking, made it to a lifeboat but Phillips died before the Carpathia arrived. Bride later helped transmit messages to New York from the Carpathia pertaining to the tragedy and the survivors.

minute before she slowly began to answer the helm, but the turn had only just commenced when her 46,000 tons slammed into the looming wall of ice.

The immediate response of those on the bridge was one of cautious relief. The blow had seemed minor. There had been a muted grinding noise and the starboard decks near the bow were littered with ice that had broken off as ship and iceberg passed, but there had been no sense of tremendous, calamitous impact.

Captain Smith appeared on the bridge almost immediately after the collision and, taking charge, ordered various officers and crew members to reconnoiter for a damage assessment. When the damage reports started coming back a few minutes later, the news was chilling. At least five--and possibly six--of the *Titanic's* watertight compartments were taking water. The inflow might be contained by the pumps in one or two of those compartments, but the *Titanic* was only designed to float with two compartments flooded. Thomas Andrews, who had also made his way to the bridge at the first sign of trouble, offered his grim expert's opinion on the reports: the ship was doomed. The captain asked how long she had. An hour, perhaps an hour-and-a-half, came the reply.

The suddenly crucial problem was that the watertight bulkheads did not extend up more than 10 feet above the waterline. With more than two compartments flooded, the bow of the ship would be pulled down to such an extent that the aft-most damaged compartment would eventually overflow into the one immediately aft of it, which, in turn, would overflow into the one aft of it, and so on, until the ship sank.

Meanwhile, many passengers were unaware that a collision had taken place. Those that were aware of something thought it most likely extremely minor. Even those who felt the crash and had seen the iceberg brush by doubted the seriousness of the situation. The White Star Line had never billed any of its ships as unsinkable, but most of the passengers--and even many of the crew--thought the *Olympic* and *Titanic* were. The unimaginable was now happening.

It was at this point that the lack of organization among the officers and crew began to tell. To make matters worse, Captain Smith found himself unable to exert decisive leadership during the ensuing crisis. For reasons known only to him, Smith never formally ordered the ship to be abandoned. Perhaps it was because he knew better than anyone the disparity between the number of persons on board and the lifeboat capacity available for them and wished to avoid a panic. Never-the-less, he told the officers to begin lowering boats about an hour after the collision. Without a formal order to abandon ship, however, there were few takers among the passengers for the first boats lowered. Consequently, boat after boat left the doomed liner with a fraction of its capacity of human life safely on board. The net result was that hundreds of people were needlessly doomed to go down with the ship.

Of course, as the list of the ship became more and more pronounced, it became progressively easier to find takers for the boats. Even then, however, the officers in charge refused to fill them. They were afraid the boats would buckle if loaded to their rated capacity. It wasn't until the last 45 minutes or so, when only a handful of boats remained, that they were sent down the sides with anything like their full capacity.

Unable for whatever reason to do much for his ship or its passengers and crew, the captain seems to have been primarily concerned with getting help. At 12:15, he ordered Phillips and his assistant, Harold Bride, to begin sending distress messages. Another tantalizing possibility was presented by a ship apparently sitting five or ten miles away on the horizon. The officers on the bridge of the *Titanic* could see what looked like a light or lights, but had no idea who or what it was. Smith had the wireless room try to reach it. There was no response. He ordered the morse lamp to be used from the bridge. Still, no response. Around 12:45, the first of the *Titanic's* distress rockets were fired. Over the next hour-and-a-half, a total of eight rockets were sent up in a final desperate attempt to reach the mystery ship, but the ship never responded.

Other ships were taking notice, however. The *Titanic's* wireless distress calls had been picked up by a number of liners, including the *Olympic*, which was steaming eastward, but unfortunately too far away to do more than lend its powerful transmitter to relay the messages. One of the ships was fairly close, at only 58 miles: the 13,564 ton Cunard liner *Carpathia*. Although the Cunard and White Star companies were great commercial rivals, all rivalries ended when a ship was in trouble at sea. The *Carpathia's* captain, Arthur Rostron, gravely read the wireless message from the *Titanic*, then sprang into action. Without a moment's hesitation, he ordered his ship turned around and headed at full speed toward the *Titanic's* stated position. He then reeled off a list of orders to his officers and crew to instruct them how to prepare to assist the survivors when they reached the *Titanic*. Finally, with the *Titanic's* fate in mind, he redoubled the look-out,

Some of the notables on the Titanic, going clockwise from the top left, included: J. Bruce Ismay, the Managing Director of the White Star Line; the noted author, W. T. Stead; philanthropist Isidor Strauss and his wife; Lady Duff Gordon, a leading figure in British society; Mrs. John Jacob Astor, the young bride of a scion of New York society; industrialist Ben Guggenheim; John Jacob Astor; and Major Archie Butt, advisor to President Taft. J. P. Morgan, who controlled International Mercantile Marine, the conglomerate that owned White Star, took ill and cancelled out. Of those pictured, only Lady Duff Gordon, Mrs. Astor and Ismay survived. Mrs. Strauss was offered a seat in a lifeboat, but refused so she could die with her husband. John Jacob Astor tried to accompany his wife, citing her "delicate condition" (she was pregnant), but was turned away. He died when the #1 funnel crashed onto the right wing bridge. Ben Guggenheim stoically put on his finest evening attire to await the end. Sir Cosmo and Lady Duff Gordon had other ideas. They all but commandeered their own lifeboat, which left the ship with 12 people out of a rated capacity of 40, and then refused to help those struggling in the water. It was rumored that Sir Cosmo had bribed the lifeboat crew not to row back. He insisted it had only been a tip but was later issued a mild reprimand by Lord Mersey who thought he might have shown a little more initiative. The Duff Gordons were practically ruined socially by the stigma.

On this page appear two contemporary renderings of the Titanic disaster. At the top appears the popular view of the collision, with the iceberg making a tremendous gash down the starboard side of the ship. Of course, it did not really happen that way. Damage of that magnitude would have sunk the ship within minutes. The iceberg actually did a sort of bump-and-grind along the side of the ship, poking a hole here, buckling a few plates there, and so on. The net result was a fatal amount of damage, but there was no 300 foot gash. This particular illustration appeared in a popular book about the disaster published in 1912 in time to cash in on the disaster mania. The title was, "The Sinking of the Titanic and Great Sea Disasters." The title page assured readers that this was "the only authoritative book" about the tragedy. The depictiion of the sinking, below, comes from another popular book of the period, "The Story of the Wreck of the Titanic, The Ocean's Greatest Disaster." The preface is dated May, 13, 1912. The publishers of the first book weren't so lazy; they went to press in April. Both books abound with photos and drawings of the Olympic erroneously identified as the Titanic.

stationing additional men at the bows, the crow's nest and on the bridge. He was determined to help, but equally determined that the icebergs would not claim a second victim that night.

Meanwhile, on board the *Titanic*, the situation was growing progressively worse. As the bow sank lower and lower into the dark Atlantic, then, finally, disappeared from view around 1:15, the passengers and crew began to come to terms with their individual fates. For a fortunate few, there were seats in the lifeboats. Others jumped into the icy water in anticipation of the end, clinging to whatever they could, hoping to make it to one of the lifeboats. Most, however, remained behind in the deceptive security of the sloping decks.

It was almost possible to believe that the ship would somehow survive. The lights still shone brightly; in fact, it seemed as if every light on board the ship was brilliantly aglow. In the gymnasium, instructors helped passengers use the equipment. In the first class smoking room, drinks were "on the house." On an upper deck, the orchestra continued to play, featuring a selection of cheerful tunes. Only the creak of the remaining lifeboats being lowered in their davits and the relentless advance of the black waters up the sloping decks predicted the horror that was about to ensue.

There has been as much debate through the years over what the orchestra was playing as over any other aspect of the tragedy. The image of the orchestra playing *Nearer My God to Thee* as the ship prepared for its final plunge is so deeply ingrained in the public's mind that it seems futile to suggest otherwise. Never-the-less, there is no reliable eyewitness evidence to support this. Nearly all the survivors who spoke of the orchestra remembered a stream of spritely popular airs of the day: rags, waltzes and music hall comic songs. The purpose of the music, after all, was to bolster peoples spirits, not traumatize them with foreshadowings of doom.

The orchestra members took up a position near the entrance to the first class lounge around 12:15 and ended up on the Boat Deck. By 2:00 they had probably stopped playing if only because the slope of the deck was becoming too extreme to set up their chairs and music stands. So the final answer to, "What was the orchestra playing when the ship went down?," is: Nothing at all. The orchestra members were swimming for dear life with most everyone else and, sadly, not one of the eight musicians survived.

There were many other tales of bravery and heroism in those early morning hours. One of the most touching vignettes was of Mrs. Strauss refusing a seat in a lifeboat so she could die with her husband. Many men, including Isidor Strauss and George Widener, refused to enter the boats so that women and children could be saved instead. Perhaps the most remarkable story was that of Benjamin Guggenheim. He retired to his stateroom to dress in his finest evening clothes, then went up on deck to die, saying to a steward:

I think there is grave doubt that the men will get off. I am willing to remain and play the man's game if there are not enough boats for more than the women and children. I won't die here like a beast. Tell my wife...I played the game out straight and to the end. No woman shall be left aboard this ship because Ben Guggenheim is a coward.

On the other hand, there were tales of cowardice and selfishness, as in the case of Sir Cosmo and Lady Duff Gordon, who all but commandeered lifeboat #1 for themselves and Lady Duff's secretary. The boat, designed for 40, finally left the ship with 12, making it the worst case of underfilling that night. Moreover, Sir Cosmo and Lady Duff refused to return to pick up more survivors after the ship went down. The British inquiry took the extraordinary step of issuing a rebuke (however mild) to Sir Cosmo over his conduct. Well, gentlemen only go so far in reproaching other gentlemen.

At 2:05, the last lifeboat departed. At 2:17, the stern suddenly rose into the air until it was nearly vertical against the starlit sky. As it did so, the freight, and anything else movable, broke loose all at once and fell toward the bows with a tremendous, thundering crash. While this transpired, the lights on board flickered and went out, then came on again in an eerie red glow, then flickered out for the last time. The stern of the ship then stood like a black, sinister finger pointed heavenward and hung in that incredible position for at least a minute before settling back slightly and disappearing from view. It was 2:20 a.m.

The survivors, to a man, reported that the ensuing cries of those 1,500 souls struggling in the frigid waters formed the most nightmarish, heart-rending and utterly unforgettable sound they had ever heard. The hideous cacophony continued for perhaps an hour, slowly diminishing as the victims one-by-one succumbed to their fate. Throughout that terrible hour, none of the lifeboats returned to help.

The first, tentative rays of dawn were creeping over the eastern horizon when the *Carpathia* approached the

The illustration appearing to the right is taken from a 1912 periodical. The title is, "Women and Children First." It is fairly accurate. The lifeboat is being laboriously, and none-too-steadily, lowered from the Boat Deck on down past the Promenade Deck. There, a fortunate lady is being helped into it by a male companion who, we presume, will then step back onto the deck of the doomed ship glad to meet his fate like a man. In fact, there were no boats that went away loaded entirely with women and children. While there were many men-- and a few women, too-- who bravely chose death, there were just as many who missed no chance to hop into the nearest available lifeboat. The lifeboat here is a little too small. The standard lifeboats were rated for 65 persons. The best feature of this picture is the feeling of barely controlled chaos that it conveys.

CUNARD R.M.S "CARPATHIA"

Titanic's final radioed position. Captain Rostron ordered rockets to be fired to let the ship know help was near. When the increasing light of day finally distinguished sea from sky, all that greeted the *Carpathia* was a pathetic little fleet of lifeboats--everything that remained of the largest liner in the world.

On the facing page, steamship travel was a business with schedules and bookings and all the trouble that went with trying to keep thousands of passengers moving smoothly through the system. The International Mercantile Marine group (IMM) controlled the seven lines listed on this published schedule (far right inset) which listed all voyages from New York to Europe, including the return leg of the Titanic's maiden voyage on April 20th (see background). If the company had trouble keeping it all straight, the travel agents really had problems because they were dealing with a wide variety of companies. When the Olympic lost a propeller blade, it forced thousands of cancellations, such as the one in this letter from a Scottish travel agent (see left inset). Among the alternatives is the maiden voyage of the Titanic, but P.W. Campbell, fortunately, was not listed as a passenger.

The Cunard liner, Carpathia, above left, was 58 miles away when it heard the Titanic's distress call. Captain Rostron immediately turned and sped toward the scene of the disaster, dodging icebergs for several hours in a futile attempt to reach the sinking White Star liner. For his efforts he became an international hero. In fact, the Titanic disaster was the turning point in Rostron's career. He had been with Cunard for 17 years, but had only spent the previous two as a master. The Carpathia didn't amount to much, either, as Cunard liners went. Launched in 1902, by 1912 she was being used in the less important Mediterranean service. By 1915, however, Rostron had risen to command of the Mauretania, one of the two most prestigious commands in the Cunard fleet (the other being the Lusitania, the Mauretania's sister). Rostron retained command of the "Mary" until 1926. In 1928, he was given the much larger Berengaria, which had started out as the German liner, Imperator. By this point, Rostron was the commodore of the entire Cunard fleet. He retired in 1931, wrote his memoirs and died in 1940. The Carpathia had a much briefer life after the Titanic. She was torpedoed in July, 1918--in the last days of World War I--and sank about 170 miles from Bishop's Rock.

Above right, lifeboat #6 approaches the side of the Carpathia. This lifeboat contained the celebrated Molly Brown, who, by this point, had definitely established that she, if not the Titanic, was unsinkable. It hadn't been easy after the ship went down. The water was a frigid 28 degrees, making survival impossible for those in the water, lifebelted or not. Collapsibles A and B had been washed free as the ship plunged--with A swamped and B overturned--and became focal points for the strongest swimmers. Soon, both were weighted down with soaked, exhausted humanity. Most of the other lifeboats had put as much distance as possible between themselves and the ship, fearing the suction as she went down or the bedlam of those frantic souls in the water. Now that she was gone, a few of the survivors began to suggest that the boats might go back to save some of the less fortunate passengers and crew swimming desperately over the ship's grave. Invariably, those who suggested going back were quickly shouted down. Only lifeboat #14, under the command of Fifth Officer Lowe, actually returned--and he waited about an hour until the crowd had "thinned out." That it had; he only found four people still alive and one of them died before the Carpathia arrived on the scene.

Date	Day	Time	Ship	Line	From	To	Via	Rate1	Rate2
Apr. 2	Tuesday	..	Cymric	White Star	Boston	Liverpool	Queenstown		
Apr. 4	Thursday	Noon	Adriatic	White Star	New York	Liverpool	Queenstown	110 00	57 50
Apr. 6	Saturday		OLYMPIC (new)	White Star	New York	Southampton	Plymouth-Cherb'g	130 00	†65 00
Apr. 6	Saturday	9.30 a.m.	St Paul	American	New York	Southampton	Plymouth-Cherb'g	95 00	*52 50
Apr. 6	Saturday	10.00 a.m.	Finland	Red Star	New York	Antwerp	Dover	85 00	55 00
Apr. 6	Saturday	10.30 a.m.	Minnehaha	Atlantic Trans.	New York	London		85 00	
Apr. 6	Saturday	10.00 a.m.	Merion	American	Phila.	Liverpool	Queenstown	....	50 00
Apr. 6	Saturday	10.00 a.m.	Canada	W.S.-Dominion	Portland	Liverpool		....	50 00
Apr. 11	Thursday	Noon	Baltic	White Star	New York	Liverpool	Queenstown	100 00	55 00
Apr. 12	Friday	10.00 a.m.	Menominee	Red Star	Phila.	Antwerp			55 00
Apr. 13	Saturday	Noon	Oceanic	White Star	New York	Southampton	Plymouth-Cherb'g		†57 50
Apr. 13	Saturday	9.30 a.m.	St Louis	American	New York	Southampton	Plymouth-Cherb'g		*52 50
Apr. 13	Saturday	10.00 a.m.	Vaderland	Red Star	New York	Antwerp	Dover		
Apr. 13	Saturday	8.00 a.m.	Minnewaska	Atlantic Trans.	New York	London			
Apr. 13	Saturday	10.00 a.m.	Megantic	W.S.-Dominion	Portland	Liverpool			
Apr. 18	Thursday	Noon	Cedric	White Star	New York	Liverpool	Queenstown		
Apr. 20	Saturday	..	TITANIC (new)	White Star	New York	Southampton	Plymouth-Cherb'g		
Apr. 20	Saturday	9.30 a.m.	Philadelphia	American	New York	Southampton	Plymouth-Cherb'g		
Apr. 20	Saturday	10.00 a.m.	Lapland	Red Star	New York	Antwerp	Dover		
Apr. 20	Saturday	10.00 a.m.	Teutonic	W.S.-Dominion	Portland	Liverpool			
Apr. 23	Tuesday	..	Majestic	White Star	Boston	Liverpool	Queenstown		
Apr. 25	Thursday	Noon	Celtic	White Star	New York	Liverpool	Queenstown		
Apr. 26	Friday	10.00 a.m.	Manitou	Red Star	Phila.	Antwerp			
Apr. 27	Saturday	..	OLYMPIC (new)	White Star	New York	Southampton	Plymouth-Cherb'		
Apr. 27	Saturday	9.30 a.m.	New York	American	New York	Southampton	Plymouth-Cherb'		
Apr. 27	Saturday	10.00 a.m.	Kroonland	Red Star	New York	Antwerp	Dover		
Apr. 27	Saturday	8.00 a.m.	Minneapolis	Atlantic Trans.	New York	London			
Apr. 27	Saturday	5.00 p.m.	Canopic	White Star	Boston	Mediterranean	‡Az'rs-Madeira		
Apr. 27	Saturday	10.00 a.m.	Haverford	American	Phila.	Liverpool	Queenstown		
Apr. 27	Saturday	10.00 a.m.	Lau—	W S.-Dominion	Portland	Liverpool			
Apr. 30	Tuesday			White Star	Boston	Liverpool	Queenstown		
May 2	Thursday			White Star	New York	Liverpool	Queenstown		
May 4	Sat—			White Star	New York	Southampton	Plymouth-Ch		
May —				American	New York	Southampton	Plymouth-Ch		
				Red Star	New York	Antwerp	Dover		
				Atlantic Trans.	New York	London			
				American	Phila.	Liverpool	Queenstown		
				W.S.-Dominion	Montreal	Liverpool	Quebec		
				White Star	Boston	Liverpool	Queenstow		
				White Star	New York	Mediterranean	‡Az'rs-Ma		
				White Star	New York	Liverpool	Queenstow		
				Red Star	Phila.	Antwerp			
				White Star	New York	Southampton	Plymout'		
				American	Phila.	Liverpool	Queenstow		
				American	New York	Southampton	Plymou—		
				Red Star	New York	Antwerp	Dover		
				Atlantic Trans.	New York	London			
				W.S.-Dominion	Montreal	Liverpool	Quebec		
				White Star	New York	Liverpool	Queen		
				White Star	New York	Southampton	Plym		
				American	New York	Southampton	Plym		
				Red Star	New York	Antwerp	Dove		
				Atlantic Trans.	New York	London			
				W.S.-Dominion	Montreal	Liverpool	Que		
				White Star	Boston	Liverpool	Qu		
				White Star	New York	Liverpool	Qu		
				Red Star	Phila.	Antwerp			
				White Star	New York	Southampton	P		
				American	New York	Southampton	P		
				Red Star	New York	Antwerp			
				Atlantic Trans.	New York	London			
				W.S.-Dominion	Phila.	Liverpool			
					Montreal	Liverpool			
				White Star	Boston	Liverpool			
				White Star	New York	Liverpool			
				White Star	New York	Southampton			
				American	New York	Southampton			
				Red Star	New York	Antwerp			
				Atlantic Trans.	New York	London			
				W.S.-Dominion	Montreal	Liverpool	Plymouth		
							Dover		
				White Star	Boston	Mediterranean	‡Azores,Giblt'r,etc.	85 00	
					Phila.	Liverpool	Queenstown	....	55 00
..W.S.-Dominion					Montreal	Liverpool	Quebec	92 50	53 75
				White Star	New York	Liverpool	Queenstown	100 00	55 00
				White Star	New York	Southampton	Plymouth-Cherb'g	110 00	†57 50
—eanic				American	New York	Southampton	Plymouth-Cherb'g	95 00	
Philadelphia									

MACKAY BROS. & CO.,
Passenger and Shipping Brokers.
Foreign and Colonial Travel Ticket Agents.
Consulting Agents Colonial Settlers' Association.

PASSAGE BROKERS BY AUTHORITY OF HIS MAJESTY'S BOARD OF TRADE

Telephone 4098 Central.

EDINBURGH CHIEF OFFICE.
29, 31, 33 HANOVER STREET.
(A few doors from Princes Street)
ALSO AT BOOKING HALL, WAVERLEY STATION.
GLASGOW OFFICE:
42 ST. ENOCH SQUARE.
DUNDEE OFFICE:
4 & 6 WHITEHALL CRESCENT.
ABERDEEN OFFICE:
35A UNION STREET.
KIRKCALDY OFFICE:
260 HIGH STREET.

Cable & Telegraphic Address: "Travel, Edinburgh."
do. do. "Traverweg, Glasgow."
do. do. "Travel, Dundee."
do. do. "Worldwide, Aberdeen."
do. do. "Travel, Kirkcaldy."
Telephones: No. 4098 Edinburgh.
do. No. 4098A Edinburgh.
do. No. 12 Central, Glasgow.
do. No. 490 Dundee.
do. No. 896 Aberdeen.
do. No. 77 Kirkcaldy.
Telegraphic Codes: "A B C" & "Unicode."

District Managers
POLYTECHNIC TOURING ASSOCIATION, Ltd.

From Edinburgh Office: 29, 31, 33 Hanover Street (A few doors from Princes Street)
Hours: 9 a.m. to 8 p.m.; Saturdays, 9 a.m. to 5 p.m.

Cable and Telegraphic Address:
"TRAVEL,
EDINBURGH."

Telegraphic Codes:
"ABC" and "Unicode."

THROUGH TICKETS
issued to
CANADA,
UNITED STATES,
SOUTH AFRICA,
AUSTRALIA AND
TASMANIA,
NEW ZEALAND,
EGYPT AND PALESTINE,
INDIA AND BURMAH,
CHINA AND JAPAN,
SOUTH AND CENTRAL
AMERICA, &c., &c.

Round the World Tours.

HEALTH AND PLEASURE
TOURS AND CRUISES.

Single, Return, or Circular
Continental Tour Tickets.

WHEN REPLYING
PLEASE QUOTE
WM/CP.

6th March 1912.

P. W. Campbell Esq.,
25, Ainsley Place,
Edinburgh.

Dear Sir,

Owing to a slight accident the sailing of the
"OLYMPIC" is deferred to 3rd April, and the "OCEANIC"
will be despatched in her place on the 27th March.

We enclose lists of the other sailings, and if
you would like any change we shall be very pleased
to hear from you.

Yours faithfully,
Mackay Bro—

Mar 13 Olympic
27th Oceanic
Apl 3 Olympic
10 Titanic

TRANSATLANTIC SAILINGS

LARGEST STEAMERS IN THE WORLD
"OLYMPIC"
"TITANIC"
(LAUNCHED)

American Line
Atlantic Transport Line
Dominion Line
Leyland Line
Red Star Line
White Star Line
White Star-Dominion Line

41

No sooner had word of the disaster reached Washington than a cry went up for a formal investigation. The cry was led by Michigan's Senator William Alden Smith who, not entirely by accident, wound up heading the committee selected to look into the matter. Smith, an aggressive populist, hoped to nail the moneyed interests with some sort of culpability in the disaster. To that end, he went to meet the Carpathia in New York and practically kidnapped Bruce Ismay and the officers and crew of the Titanic. They were detained in America for weeks, first in New York and later in Washington. The committee initially set up shop in the ballroom of the elegant Waldorf-Astoria Hotel in New York. It was in that room that Bruce Ismay was first put through the ordeal of being questioned for the record. In this illustration, Ismay is seated at the end of the table, resting his head on his left hand. Senator Smith is seated on the left with his right elbow on the table while he looks down at this notes. The American inquiry was vilified in the British press and Smith was dismissed as a publicity-seeking bumpkin, but his investigation was remarkably thorough and still stands as the best record of what happened on that tragic April night.

Chapter 6. Aftermath of the Titanic Disaster

If I go to Washington, it will not be because of this story in the paper, but to tell the committee why my ship was drifting without power while the *Titanic* was rushing under full speed. It will take about ten minutes to do this. (Captain Stanley Lord of the *Californian*)

The *Carpathia* arrived on the scene at 4 o'clock in the morning on April 15th, less than two hours after the *Titanic* had made its final plunge. In so doing, Captain Rostron had dodged at least five icebergs during his ship's mad dash to the *Titanic's* final radioed position and was well on his way to becoming one of the genuine heroes of the affair.

As day broke, a fantastic sight appeared. The *Carpathia* was two or three miles east of an enormous ice field studded with huge icebergs, some 200 feet high. To the east and south were still other bergs, one of which no doubt had had a collision with a liner the night before. For four hours, the *Carpathia* maneuvered carefully among the ice locating the *Titanic's* lifeboats and retrieving the survivors. By 8:30, the last of them had been brought on board just as the *Californian* steamed up asking if she could be of help. Rostron asked her to look around for any survivors the *Carpathia* may have missed, then turned to make for New York.

The *Titanic* had carried lifeboats with enough capacity for 1,178 passengers--far fewer than the 2,201 on board and grossly inadequate to the 3,300 who *might* have been on board had she been full. Despite this, there were only 705 survivors, according to the most widely accepted current tabulation. A total of 1,502 people had gone down with the ship, including 473 who should have found places in the boats, but did not.

The precise breakdown of survivors, according to the British inquiry, was as follows:

First class: 203 saved (62%), 122 lost (38%).
Second class: 118 saved (41%), 167 lost (59%).
Third class: 178 saved (25%), 528 lost (75%).
Crew: 212 saved (24%), 673 lost (76%).

Men took a drubbing in every class, although those

in first class did somewhat better than the overall average. Only one child out of 30 was lost in either first or second class, however, compared to nearly half lost in third class (52 lost out of 109). Only 17 women out of 220 in first and second class were lost, compared to 89 out of 169 in third.

Of the well-known personages on board, few of the men survived. As the end neared, John Jacob Astor, observing the unfolding catastrophe from the right wing bridge, was killed when the first funnel came crashing down. His mangled, soot-covered body was later recovered. George Widener, Archie Butt, Ben Guggenheim, Frank Millet, W. T. Stead, Jacques Futrelle, Isidor Strauss and Henry B. Harris all perished.

The officers and crew of the *Titanic* certainly could not have been accused of failing in their ultimate duty. Those who were lost included the Captain, Chief Officer, First Officer, Sixth Officer and Chief Purser. There were reports that First Officer Murdoch, who had been on the bridge at the time of the collision, had shot himself in the final minutes, but these have never been confirmed. The Captain was seen by several witnesses swimming in the water but he never made it into one of the lifeboats and his body was never found.

Thomas Andrews, Managing Director of Harland and Wolff, had been last seen, his arms folded, lost in thought, standing in the first class smoking room. He was not among the survivors. Bruce Ismay, Managing Director of White Star, was, however, and may soon have wished he wasn't.

In their need for a scapegoat, the public, especially in America, quickly zeroed-in on Ismay. Why, people asked, was the head of the company alive and well while 1,500 of his employees and customers were at the bottom of the sea--including hundreds of women and children? Ismay hardly helped his reputation by sending a coded message from the *Carpathia* instructing White Star officials in New York to hold the *Cedric* so that he and the surviving crew members could return to England immediately. The message was intercepted and looked, to American eyes at least, like a blatant attempt to flee American jurisdiction. All sorts of horrid rumors and innuendo began swirling around Ismay. He had pressured Captain Smith to try for a speed record. He had pompously interfered with the handling of the lifeboats. He had escaped in one of the last boats disguised as a woman. None of these charges was ever substantiated, but Ismay lived under the cloud of the *Titanic* for the remainder of his life.

As soon as word of the tragedy got out, there was a tremendous outpouring of public shock, grief and anger. Newspapers the world over covered the story on page one and editorialized about its meaning. There was scarcely a pulpit in Christendom that did not feature a *Titanic*-related sermon the following Sunday. Those with an entrepreneurial bent were busy, too. An amazing variety of *Titanic* souvenirs appeared almost as suddenly as the ship had disappeared. There were special *Titanic* editions of newspapers and magazines. Postcards proliferated, most of which actually depicted the *Olympic*, *Titanic* photos being rather rare, then as now. Also offered to an eager public were lamps, plates, pins-- anything to which an image even vaguely resembling the *Titanic* could be affixed.

When the *Carpathia* neared New York on the evening of April 18th, she was greeted by a scene of sheer pandemonium. The ship was hounded by the press and the curious as soon as the harbor was reached and the bedlam at the Cunard pier was never-to-be-forgotten. Among those present were members of a special United States Senate sub-committee with subpoenas for Bruce Ismay, the officers and crew.

No sooner had the shocking news of the disaster reached the world than calls for an American investigation had begun to be heard. The ship had been American owned and there had been notable Americans lost, so it seemed fitting to many in the media and in public life that someone should move quickly to get to the bottom of the thing.

The man who grabbed the reins of investigation was a United States Senator, William Alden Smith from Michigan. Even before the *Carpathia* docked, he introduced legislation to create a special Senate sub-committee to conduct an inquiry and, to no one's surprise, ended up heading it. Smith did not have the best reputation in Washington. He was a populist with a bombastic speaking style and was noted for his pugnacious and divisive manner. Indeed, he had a hidden reason for wanting the investigation. He was convinced that the moneyed interests had likely criminal liability the survivors and the families of victims could have exploited to collect damages. To this end, he practically kidnapped Bruce Ismay, the surviving officers and crew and held them against their will for weeks, first in New York and, later, in Washington. Smith's investigation was brutally attacked in the British press and even in some of the American newspapers. Smith himself was widely vilified as a publicity-seeking ignoramus.

Still, although Smith was never able to prove his hidden agenda, the American inquiry served an invaluable purpose. For all his brazen insensitivity, Smith did manage to get a sworn record of the disaster from the officers and crew of the *Titanic*, to say nothing of Ismay, within days of the sinking--before they had a chance to polish their stories. He also was the first to get to Captain Stanley Lord of the *Californian*. Because of this, the American inquiry is the best record of the order of events on that fatal night.

The later British Inquiry was technically the Wreck Commissioner's Court. It was headed by Lord Mersey, who subsequently chaired a similar investigation into the loss the the *Lusitania*. The British inquiry was more interested in the mechanics of the disaster, i.e., the structure of the ship, the nature of the damage, the prevailing navigational practices, etc. While the inquiry in America had relied primarily on anecdotal evidence, Lord Mersey questioned a long line of expert witnesses, including those from the company and builder.

Despite their different approaches, and the ridicule heaped on the American inquiry in the British press, the two investigations came to remarkably similar conclusions. Both cited design deficiencies in the ship-- especially with respect to the lifeboats, both condemned prevalent navigational practices, both cleared the White Star Line of any outrageous misdeeds, both cleared Bruce Ismay of any personal wrongdoing, both acknowledged that the *Titanic* was not trying for any sort of speed record, both concluded that the damage to the ship was so severe that nothing could have been done to save her, both called for a radical revision of laws regulating ocean-going passenger ships, both called for 24-hour wireless operations on board liners, both called for more and better lifeboat drills, and, finally, both fingered Captain Lord of the *Californian* for having stood by and done nothing.

A major difference in the two reports surrounded Captain Smith. The British inquiry faulted his practices, but found him blameless. Mersey declared:

> I am not able to blame Captain Smith...He was only doing that which other skilled men would have done in the same position...He made a mistake, a very grievous mistake, but one in which, in the face of the practice and of past experience, negligence cannot be said to have had any part; and, in the absence of negligence it is, in my opinion, impossible to fix Captain Smith with blame.

The Americans saw the matter a bit differently.

Senator Smith concluded:

Captain Smith knew the sea, and his clear eye and steady hand had often guided his ship through dangerous paths...His indifference to danger was one of the direct and contributing causes to this unnecessary tragedy...Overconfidence seems to have dulled the faculties usually so alert.

Few modern-day *Titanic* scholars would disagree with Senator Smith's assessment. On the other hand, Second Officer Lightoller, the *Titanic's* ranking surviving officer, had his own succinct explanation for why the tragedy had taken place:

Of course, we know now the extraordinary combination of circumstances that existed at that time which you would not meet again in 100 years; that they should all have existed just on that particular night shows, of course, that everything was against us.

Well...not exactly. This explanation made it sound as if the whole terrible thing had been unavoidable, as if the careless navigation in ice-infested waters, the sloppy loading of the boats and the basic design shortcomings of the ship herself had all been decisions to which no reasonable responsibility or blame could have been attached. A dispassionate examination of the evidence indicates several contributing causes of the disaster:

The Navigation

The ship was steaming at what can only be fairly described as a reckless speed through waters known to be ice-infested, especially given the prevailing weather conditions. There was no moon that night to illuminate icebergs and no roughness to the sea itself that might have outlined them with whitecaps. Thus, the fatal iceberg was unusually hard to see at a safe distance.

The fact that Captain Smith had no organized system for posting the six known ice warnings received by his ship only compounded the pervasive laxity on

Left, the day is April 2, 1912, and the Titanic is moving down Belfast Lough to begin her brief sea trials. The tugs are getting ready to cast off and in a few moments the Titanic will be on her own for the first time. The Titanic's trials were not, however, nearly as extensive as those given the Olympic.

the *Titanic's* bridge throughout the final day. Every officer on the bridge that day knew they were approaching ice, yet no one did anything about it-- including Captain Smith.

The prevailing navigational practice of the time did not call for slowing down in waters suspected of being ice-infested. Instead, most masters simply increased their look-outs--something which Captain Smith had not done either. The practice of continuing at speed in dangerous waters made sense when ships were slower and more maneuverable. A 500 foot ship going 13 knots may have no need to slow down for ice, but a 900 foot ship going 21 knots has increased its vulnerability by some quantum factor.

To compound matters, the course itself was dangerous. The standard steamship lanes in winter months were too far north for the interests of safety. The routes were shorter that way, but placed all ships at special hazard for just the sort of unbroken ice packs encountered by the *Titanic*. They were subsequently moved further south.

The Evasive Action

The evasive action taken was clearly counter-productive. When the iceberg was sighted, First Officer Murdoch immediately reversed his engines. At the same time, he ordered a hard turn to port. He was, he explained to Captain Smith who appeared on the bridge moments after the collision, attempting to "port around" the berg, i.e., attempting to swing the vast bulk of the ship around the iceberg, using the berg as the apex but without coming into contact with it. It obviously didn't work. Part of the problem may have been the sheer momentum of a 46,000 ton ship, part may have been the design of the rudder, but part may have been his choice of tactics.

By reversing engines, for example, Murdoch had to shut down the center screw, because the turbine was not reversible. In doing so, he also eliminated the propwash flowing past the rudder and diminished the rudder's effectiveness. He would have done better to have maintained his speed as he executed his turning maneuver. Ultimately, however, he would have done best to have not tried to avoid the iceberg at all, but simply rammed it head-on. That is a collision the *Titanic* could almost certainly have survived, albeit with severe damage. It would have been a hard call to make, though. (One can just hear the Monday morning quarterbacks ganging up on poor Murdoch saying,

"Look at the damage you caused! Why didn't you just try to avoid the darned thing?") So, while Murdoch's decision to try to port around the berg may have been perfectly understandable, it was undoubtedly the wrong action to take under the circumstances.

The Damage

The exact nature of the damage has been a subject of public fascination, to say nothing of continuing debate among the experts, almost since the news broke in 1912. One of the real regrets scholars have regarding the recent discovery and exploration of the wreck is that it has shed so little light on this issue (see Chapter 7).

The typical image of the damage is one of a huge, continuous gash running perhaps 300 feet along the starboard side. Damage of that magnitude would have sunk the ship within minutes, however, much as happened with the *Empress of Ireland* and the *Lusitania*. The fact that the *Titanic* remained afloat for nearly three hours, indicates the presence of a more subtle, though no less fatal, kind of havoc.

Edward Wilding, the architect at Harland and Wolff who was primarily responsible for the *Titanic*, estimated the area of damage at 249 feet--the length of the ship from the bow back to a point two feet into Boiler Room #5. Using reliable eye witness accounts, he calculated the amount of water that had entered the ship in the first 40 minutes after the crash at 16,000 cubic feet. He then worked backward to determine the size hole that would produce such a result. His answer: 12 square feet. That, in turn, would have produced a continuous gash about three-quarters-of-an-inch wide! Obviously, that did not happen. The berg penetrated more than 3 feet into hold #1, leaving an enormous hole. In Boiler Room #5, the apparent damage was fairly minor and could easily have been controlled by the pumps. The damage was most likely more severe than it seemed, though.

Wilding himself noted that the damage running back from Boiler Room #6 into Boiler Room #5 undoubtedly also damaged the watertight bulkhead standing between them. Sure enough, about an hour after the collision there was a sudden rush of water into Boiler Room #5 that forced workmen to abandon the pumps and run for dear life. Something gave way and it was probably all or part of the bulkhead.

Further aft, Boiler Room #4 also seems to have been damaged. Around an hour and 40 minutes after the collision, water began rising up from below. The flow was more than the pumps could handle and must have come from some sort of hidden damage to the double bottom. If so, this would make Boiler Room #4 the *seventh* watertight compartment breeched and raise the level of violence to a point that renders ludicrous any suggestions of remedial action that Captain Smith might have taken.

Evidently, the iceberg did a sort of bump-and-grind along the side of the ship, gashing a big hole here, poking a little hole there, fracturing this bulkhead, buckling those plates, and so on. The cumulative result was Wilding's 12 square feet of damage, but not in the form of a continuous gash. Especially in light of what happened in Boiler Room #4, however, it seems clear that the structural integrity of the hull itself was lethally compromised in some fundamental--and absolutely frightful--way.

Could Captain Smith have done anything to save his ship? No. The damage was simply overwhelming.

Could he have done anything to have slowed the sinking? It has been suggested that he might have reopened the watertight doors to allow the ship to fill more evenly and, thus, settle on an even keel. This probably would have delayed the end by a few minutes, although by how much is pure speculation. It seems doubtful that a matter of minutes, or even an hour, would have saved any lives. Two or three more hours would have made an enormous difference--the *Carpathia* would have been on the scene by then--but anything less than that couldn't have meant much.

The Lifeboats

The disparity between people and lifeboat capacity was an obvious issue at the British and American hearings. The popular wisdom for 75 years has been that the lack of sufficient lifeboat capacity was the main factor in the huge loss of life.

The Board of Trade regulation covering lifeboats had been enacted in 1894 and required ships of more than 10,000 tons to carry sufficient boats for 962 persons--or, 16 boats of the size carried by the *Titanic*. The *Titanic* was originally designed for 48 lifeboats. She was only fitted with 20, however, with a rated capacity of 1,178 (still 22% above the legal requirement), but 4 of those boats were collapsibles of only marginal use. On the fatal night, she needed at least 37 standard-size boats--assuming they had been filled to capacity, which they weren't until the very end.

In a related matter at both hearings into the tragedy,

White Star officials heatedly denied that there had been discrimination or restrictions of any kind against lower class passengers regarding access to the boats. Both inquiries looked into the question and both supported the company's position. Still, a far higher percentage of first class passengers numbered among the survivors than did those travelling second or third class.

A subtle problem confronted second and, especially, third class passengers. Since the order to abandon ship had never been given, word of the disaster followed the "trickle down" theory with passengers either stumbling across the fact or hearing of it through word of mouth. The way the ship was laid out, both the bridge and most of the Boat Deck were technically in first class territory. First class passengers were a pampered lot and mingled freely with the officers of the ship. Those first class passengers who failed to garner the news in that fashion, couldn't help noticing the boats being lowered. The simple truth is that first class passengers, by and large, learned of the danger first, had the lifeboats close at hand, and, thus, had more time to act. By the time the news filtered down to the other classes, many of the already scarce boats were gone.

The real enemies that night, however, were lack of time and poor leadership, not the shortage of lifeboats. Even if they had had the number lifeboats they needed, it is impossible to see how they could have launched them. To begin with, Captain Smith waited an hour before ordering the first boats lowered, thus cutting the launching time available by at least a third and, when the need arose, there were no organized boat crews. Officers had not been assigned to specific boat stations until the ship reached open sea, nor were passengers ever assigned to specific boats (which, in a sense, was understandable given the fact that there were not nearly enough boats to go around). There had never been a full-scale boat drill at sea. One had been scheduled during the voyage, then cancelled. The net result was that no one knew where to go or what to do. Instead of launching several boats concurrently, the boats were laboriously handled one by one. The *ad hoc* boat crews worked feverishly almost until the ship up-ended. Indeed, the 20th and last boat, one of the collapsibles, was sent off with sea water washing knee-deep across the Boat Deck. Under the prevailing circumstances, a *Titanic* fitted with the 48 lifeboats originally proposed would probably have gone down with more than half those boats still hanging from their davits--and the death toll would likely not have been greatly affected.

The death toll was compounded by the lack of

training and experience of the officers who did not know that the lifeboats could be sent down the sides loaded to their rated capacity. No one had told them that Harland and Wolff had test-lowered the boats at full capacity and found them perfectly safe. Thus, most of the boats were only partially filled.

So, as to the question of lifeboats, *if* there had been a sufficient number of trained boat crews and *if* Captain Smith had exerted timely leadership, then the shortage of boats would have hurt. As it was, it probably didn't make much difference.

Structural Shortcomings

The structural design may have contributed to the collision. There was some debate over the effectiveness of the rudder. Had it been larger, the ship might have been more maneuverable.

The structural design of the ship was faulty in other ways. The double bottom should have been run up the sides at least to a point above the waterline. Similarly, the watertight bulkheads, which only extended 10 feet above the waterline, should have extended upward another 20 feet or so. Longitudinal watertight bulkheads, in addition to the transverse bulkheads, would also have helped.

The Unsinkable Ship?

Both inquiries, but especially the American one, delved into the question of whether the White Star Line had advertised the *Olympic* and *Titanic* as being unsinkable. Both concluded that it had not, but this remains one of the great, enduring myths of the tragedy.

One searches White Star literature and advertisements of the period in vain for any such claim. It never passed their lips. Of course, Harland and Wolff had very responsibly built the two ships to withstand the worst accident they or the company could imagine: two compartments flooded. If they could have imagined a six-compartment catastrophe such as befell the *Titanic*, they would have made allowances. So, it would be fair to say that the builders and the company no doubt considered the ship unsinkable in the very practical sense that it was built to withstand the worst they could conceive. That is not the same as saying they thought the ship could not be sunk, at least in the theoretical sense.

On the other hand, there were certainly those who did think the new ships unsinkable. The prestigious industry trade journal, *The Shipbuilder*, referred to them in print as being "practically unsinkable"--not quite a definitive statement, but close enough. Other less knowledgeable newspapers and magazines spoke on the subject without *The Shipbuilder's* professional reserve. More to the point, many, if not most, of the passengers and crew on board the *Titanic* believed the claim, no matter what the source. The story--probably true for once--is often told of a crewman having reassured a nervous passenger prior to the departure from Southampton, saying, "God himself could not sink this ship!" This opinion likely extended as far up the chain of command as Captain Smith himself. In an interview in 1906, when he commanded the *Adriatic*, a ship half the size of the *Titanic*, he had said:

> I cannot imagine any condition which would cause a ship to founder. I cannot conceive of any vital disaster happening to this vessel [the *Adriatic*]. Modern shipbuilding has gone beyond that.

It was a misconception that was destined to cost Captain Smith his life.

The *Californian*

Captain Smith was not the only ship's master who met his doom that night. For all practical purposes, Captain Stanley Lord of the *Californian* might have just as well have gone down with him. No sooner had the *Californian* docked in Boston than disgruntled crewmen began talking to the newspapers about their ship having sighted the *Titanic* that night, seen the distress rockets and done nothing.

Captain Lord was interrogated at length by both American and British inquiries and he quickly discovered that gratuitous attacks on Captain Smith were not going to be enough to get him off the hook (see the opening quotation in this chapter). His rather lame excuse was that he thought the rockets seen by the *Californian* had been company signals of some sort, rather than distress rockets. He was alone in that contention. All the other officers and crew on the *Californian* that night thought they were distress rockets. Both American and British inquiries condemned

In the photograph, right, the Titanic eases away from its Southampton pier on its maiden voyage. Aft, the open gangway door of the crew entrance is visible.

Lord's conduct in the strongest possible terms. The American tribunal, for instance, concluded:

> [The *Californian*] failed to respond...in accordance with the dictates of humanity, international usage, and the requirements of law.

Lord Mersey was equally direct:

> There are inconsistencies and contradictions in the story as told by different witnesses, but the truth of the matter is plain...When she first saw the rockets, the *Californian* could have pushed through the ice to open water without any serious risk and so have come to the assistance of the *Titanic*. Had she done so, she might have saved many, if not all of the lives that were lost.

Captain Lord has always had a few vociferous defenders, known among *Titanic* scholars as Lordites. They do not deny that the *Californian* saw a ship that night that appeared about the same time the *Titanic* struck the iceberg and disappeared about the time the *Titanic* sank. They do not deny that the *Titanic* fired eight white distress rockets at various times and that the *Californian* saw eight distress rockets of the same color and at the same times. Their basic argument is that there was a third ship between the *Californian* and the *Titanic*. The fact that this third ship has never been found, that no one on board the *Titanic* saw any other ship firing rockets nearby, that the credible positions of both ships makes it highly unlikely they were out of visual range of each other (let alone of each other's rockets) during the sinking--all of these facts are tortuously explained away in one form or another by the Lordites. The rockets, though, are the key. The *Titanic* fired them--and a whole list of people on board the *Californian* saw them. Even if the Lordites are correct and there was a third ship firing the distress rockets seen by the *Californian*, Captain Lord *still* did nothing. When you get right down to it, their defense is that Captain Lord abandoned some *other* ship to its doom. Some defense! The case against the *Californian* is overwhelming and, considering all the available evidence, Captain Lord's dereliction is the only plausible conclusion.

As Walter Lord, perhaps the most noted of American *Titanic* scholars, has written:

> [The Lordites] come across as energetic,

resourceful--and highly selective in presenting their evidence...They can say what they like, but they can't get away from those rockets.

In the wake of the *Titanic* scandal, the Leyland line demanded Lord's resignation. He went back to sea during World War I and served for a time with a lesser line, but retired in 1927 while still a relatively young man, citing poor health. When he died in 1962 at the age of 84, he was still stoutly protesting his innocence.

Conclusions

The shortage of lifeboats, the design of the watertight bulkheads, the weather, the course and so on, all played a role in the *Titanic* disaster. In the final analysis, though, if Captain Smith had done a responsible job of navigation on that fateful Sunday, the tragedy would never have occurred. If he had paid attention to the ice warnings, if he had cut his speed and increased his look-outs, there would not have been a collision--certainly not of the tragic scope that resulted. He would have gone into a dignified retirement and the *Titanic* would be forgotten today by all but a few dyed-in-the-wool steamship buffs.

After the collision, Captain Smith compounded the tragedy by his inexplicable delay in ordering the boats to be launched and in his failure to formally order the ship to be abandoned. It is possible that the magnitude of the crisis simply immobilized him. By his own words, he had never in over 40 years at sea been "in a predicament that threatened to end in disaster of any sort." Perhaps he simply didn't know what to do. Regardless, Captain Smith's careless navigation was the proximate cause of the collision and, after the collision, his lack of leadership almost certainly prevented several hundred people from escaping with their lives. Even so, a modicum of alertness to duty on the part of Captain Lord could in all likelihood have resulted in the salvation of many or all of the victims.

This was a tragedy that need not have happened.

Epilogue

The aftermath of the *Titanic's* sinking saw a number of positive developments in the maritime industry. Chief among these was the International

Left, two disaster cards, one German, one French. Typical with the genre, the latter shows the Olympic.

Conference for the Safety of Life at Sea, convened in London in 1913. The conference adopted a number of measures to ensure that a disaster comparable to that of the *Titanic* would not recur:

All ocean-going ships were required to carry lifeboats with sufficient capacity for all passengers and crew on board. Masters of ships were required to alter course or reduce speed when encountering ice, or even reports of ice, at night. The use of distress signals, rockets, etc., for any purpose other than genuine distress was strictly prohibited. Wireless sets were mandated on all ships and sending power was to be increased. An international ice patrol was created, with responsibility for its operation offered to the United States. This patrol soon became the United States Coast Guard. In commemoration of the event that led to its creation, every year on April 15th the Coast Guard drops a wreath at the *Titanic's* final radioed position.

The U.S. Congress had already enacted a sweeping piece of maritime regulatory legislation, known as the Smith Bill. Senator Smith had not rested at the close of his official inquiry; he had proceeded to draft a stunningly comprehensive set of regulations to which any shipping line doing business in a U.S. port would have to submit. The bill was particularly heavy with safety-related regulations, covering everything from the way lifeboats were to be assigned to passengers to the design of watertight bulkheads. It also sought to extend the provisions of American anti-trust law to steamship companies doing business in America.

Through the decades, public interest in the *Titanic* has remained remarkably high. Although it seemed to wane a bit in the 1940s, interest has actually grown in the years since. The discovery of the wreck in 1985 sent public excitement to a level not surpassed since 1912 and it shows no signs of abatement. Symptomatically, *Titanic* memorabilia that was high-priced five years ago, is staggeringly expensive today--and going up.

This was truly a universal tragedy, a watershed event in western culture. The *Titanic* was far more than just a ship; it was a symbol of a by-gone era in which material progress was considered an end in itself and a subject of almost religious devotion. The ultimate triumph of man over nature was assumed--until nature gave man his comeuppance on that cold April night.

The Fourth Estate found ways to cash in on the post-disaster mania, too. The souvenir edition put out by Britain's "Lloyd's Weekly News" was typical of the type--and the photo really is the Titanic.

Chapter 7.
Titanic Redux: Discovery

Question: How is Cleveland, Ohio, different from the Titanic? Answer: Cleveland has a better orchestra. (A contemporary popular joke)*

Almost as soon as the *Titanic* disappeared into the black waters of the North Atlantic 350 miles southeast of Newfoundland, people began talking of salvaging the wreck. Most of this talk was just that--talk. The most daunting obstacle was simply finding it. The *Titanic* was known to lie in about two miles of water in the least friendly ocean in the world, but its precise position was only a guess. Apart from the financial and

* For 75 years, the image of the *Titanic* has often been invoked for comparative and, frequently, humorous purposes. The above joke made the rounds among Clevelanders a few years ago when that city was approaching muncipal bankruptcy. Having grown up in the Cleveland area, I just couldn't resist including it. My sincere apologies to all my friends in Cleveland...if I still have any...

logistical problems entailed, until five or ten years ago the technology simply did not exist to make such a search even remotely practical. The unsinkable ship had become the undiscoverable ship.

In 1985, spurred by the development of advanced sonar technology and remarkable deep-diving robot submersibles, a joint U.S.-French expedition set out to do the impossible. The search used the *Alvin* submersible developed in 1964 by the Woods Hole Oceanographic Institution in co-operation with the U.S. Navy. The *Alvin* was improved over the years to the point where it could make dives to a depth of 13,000 feet. Moreover, the *Alvin* could carry with it a smaller robot submersible, the *Jason Jr.*, able to go places too small even for the mother ship. Dr. Robert Ballard, eventual co-leader of the expedition to the *Titanic*, realized that the capabilities of the *Alvin* made a search for the fabled liner feasible at last.

On September 1, 1985, the search succeeded. The American team, under the direction of Ballard, finally discovered the wreck of the *Titanic*. The ship is broken into three parts. There are two main sections. One consists of the forward half of the ship. The other comprises the final third, measuring forward from the stern. That leaves perhaps 10-15% of the ship missing

in the area of the third and fourth funnels. Part of this third section has reportedly been located, but not thoroughly explored. The bow and stern sections, have been exhaustively photographed and studied, however.

The bow section is in relatively good shape. The funnels are missing and much of the wood has been eaten away, but the hull and superstructure are essentially intact. The stern section, on the other hand, is in severely damaged condition and lies some distance away from the forward section with the stern turned around so that it points in the same general direction as the bow. Between the two sections lies a debris field. No human remains have been found.

There were two basic questions *Titanic* researchers hoped to have answered by the exploration of the wreck. One was the exact nature of the damage to the hull caused by the collision. The other was a convincing answer to whether she broke in two before she went down, as many witnesses had claimed.

On the first point--the precise nature of the collision damage--the exploration has been a profound disappointment. The forward half of the ship is buried in the sea bottom in such a way, and to such a depth, that extensive visual examination of the lower portion of the outer hull has been impossible. The keel is

hogged, or broken, perhaps a quarter of the way back along its length from the bow, but this could easily have transpired as the ship struck bottom--and probably did. There is no plausible explanation for why it would have happened on the surface. The testimony of survivors, together with detailed historical research, are going to have to continue to provide the answers on this subject until, and unless, a way is found to explore the lower forward hull.

It is on the second point, that the exploration has prompted spirited debate among researchers. There are three main theories as to how the ship broke in two (or three). The first holds that the ship broke in two before the final plunge. The second contends that the break-up occurred as the ship struck bottom. The third declines to accept either of the first two theories alone and seeks a synthesis of the two.

Regarding the first theory, it has been the contention of many researchers for decades that the ship broke on the surface. Sixteen survivors testified at the British and/or American inquiries that just before the ship went down they had seen the break occur between the third and fourth funnels. That particular part of the ship was a weak point in the structure. The after first class staircase penetrated from the Boat Deck all the way down to C Deck. Below that was only one deck before the reciprocating engine room was reached--the largest open space in the ship, rising all the way from the tank top up through E Deck. Thus, except for D Deck, the ship was already cut through at this point from the Boat Deck almost down to the keel. One can imagine the incredible stress that was inflicted on the hull as the stern rose out of the water prior to the final plunge--stress that the hull was never intended to bear.

Still, there are a several weak points to this first theory. To begin with, all the expert witnesses testifying in 1912 discounted it, including all the surviving officers of the ship who testified to the point. Edward Wilding, the architect from Harland and Wolff who designed the ship, insisted the hull was simply too strong to break in that fashion. The debris field also seems too confined, spanning a closely defined area between the two main sections of the ship. If the ship had broken on the surface, one would have expected the debris to be more widely scattered. Finally, if the two

The wreck of the Titanic was discovered in two main sections (and a smaller third section) by the Alvin submersible, as depicted in this artist's conception, left. In between is a debris field, but no human remains.

main sections fell independently to the bottom, they should both have hit at approximately the same speed (estimated by experts to have been 25-30 mph) and have suffered much the same damage. But, this is not the case. The bow section is relatively pristine, while the stern section is severely smashed.

The second theory, that the ship went down intact and broke at the bottom, answers many of the objections to the first theory. It is consistent with all the expert testimony that a break-up prior to the final plunge either did not, or could not, have happened. Also, no one testified that the ship broke in *three*, yet that is the way the wreck lies. Moreover, the physical evidence suggests that the ship may reversed position as she descended. In other words, she may have gone down by the bows, but, since most of her weight was in the stern where the engines were located, she could well have switched on the way down to a stern-first position. She had two miles to do this, after all. If the stern had struck first, broken off (along with that smaller, third section) and perhaps flipped end-over-end or rolled, it would explain the relative nature of the damage to the two sections as well as the spread of the debris field. It is interesting to note that the prow appears undamaged and the main mast has fallen back onto the bridge. Had the bow struck head-on with 46,000 tons of momentum behind it, it seems likely that the prow would have been severely smashed and the mast would have fallen the other way, toward the point of impact at the bows. The absence of this sort of damage strongly suggests a stern-first impact.

The third theory seeks a middle ground between the first two scenarios. This theory refuses to dismiss the remarkably consistent testimony of all those witnesses who thought they saw the break-up in the area of the third and fourth funnels--just where the ship is, in fact, broken, and where it would most likely have broken given the hull design. This theory holds that the ship began to break on the surface as the stern rose in the air but still went down as a single, albeit severely fractured, unit, switching to a stern-first position during the descent, and breaking into the three sections that exist as the stern struck bottom. The elegance of this theory is that it ties together all the evidence, both the seemingly contradictory testimony in 1912 and the physical evidence presented by the wreck itself.

Will the wreck of the *Titanic* ever be salvaged? It is feasible--and therefore possible--that items from the wreck may someday be salvaged, despite an active international campaign (in which Dr. Ballard has played

a major role) to prevent such activity. The wreck lies in international waters and is legally fair game. It seems highly improbable that the wreck itself will be brought up. It is simply too far down and in too many pieces to make any attempt to do that seem worthwhile given current technology. Still, if the *Titanic* has taught us anything, it is that nothing is impossible.

Meanwhile, there have been a steady stream of published works that have in significant ways added to our store of knowledge about the *Titanic* and her sisters. There haven't been many books that attempted to put the trio in perspective, although Roy Anderson's *White Star*, published more than 20 years ago and long out of print, was an excellent recounting of the history of the White Star Line. Nearly all the other books that have been written concentrate almost entirely on the *Titanic*.

The granddaddy of all *Titanic* books is Walter Lord's landmark work, *A Night to Remember*, first published in 1955. Still the one of the best books about the sinking of the *Titanic* for the lay reader, it is not well illustrated, but is beautifully and grippingly written. Lord's latest opus, *The Night Lives On: New Thoughts, Theories and Revelations About the Titanic*, sort of an appendix to the first, is likewise excellent.

A rival to Walter Lord's first volume is Wyn Craig Wade's recent book, *The Titanic: End of a Dream*. This book is the probably the best in print regarding the important 1912 American inquiry into the tragedy.

Another recent book is, *Titanic: Triumph and Tragedy*, by John P. Eaton and Charles A. Haas, a huge, well-illustrated volume. I have some problems with it because of their conclusions on certain issues, most prominently the affair of the *Californian*, but it is still an impressive book.

Those wanting to delve into the true minutae of the design and construction of the *Olympic* and *Titanic* cannot do better than to find a copy of the reprint of the *Olympic & Titanic* issue of *The Shipbuilder* magazine, first published at the time the *Olympic* went into service in 1911. It has been reissued a couple of times in hardcover by Patrick Stephens Ltd., a British publishing house, and is an essential for the real buff, although far too detailed for the casual reader.

There are more books coming out all the time. Most of them, gratifyingly enough, are pretty good. The *Titanic* and her sisters will no doubt be inspiring writers for decades--if not centuries--to come.

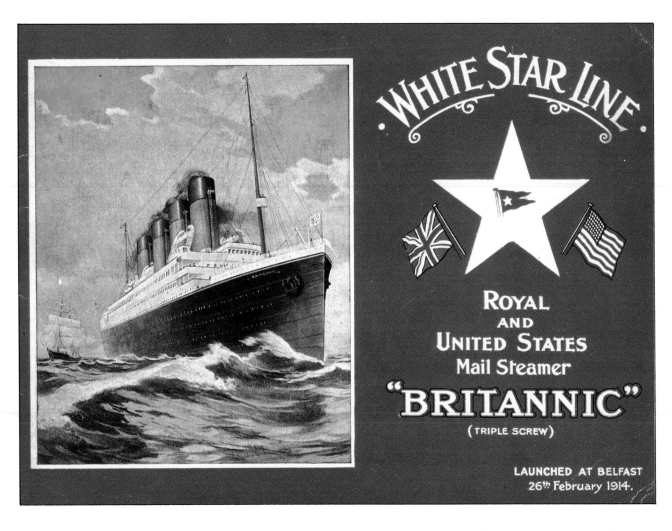

WHITE STAR LINE

ROYAL
AND
UNITED STATES
Mail Steamer
"BRITANNIC"
(TRIPLE SCREW)

LAUNCHED AT BELFAST
26th February 1914.

Chapter 8.
Titanic's Unlucky
Sister: The Story
of the Britannic

In the new "Britannic" we see, both in design and construction, as perfect a specimen of man's creative power as it is possible to conceive. (*Britannic* launch booklet)

The third of the White Star Line's unlucky trio was laid down in November, 1911, and launched on February 26, 1914. The outbreak of war in August, 1914, had fateful consequences for the new liner. Launched too late to go into service as a commercial liner, it was decided to complete her as a hospital ship. Fitting out as a passenger ship would have to come later--and, as it turned out, never.

The original name of the *Britannic* has been a source of recurring debate among steamship buffs. Many have claimed that the name initially selected for her by White Star officials was *Gigantic*. Others have cast doubt on this, seeing it as a bit of post-*Titanic* nonsense, another piece of revisionist mythology, of which there has been so much surrounding these ships. The fact is, however, that *Gigantic* was, indeed, the original name--at least the available evidence clearly points in that direction.

Although authentic White Star documentation is

lacking, published reports at the time of the *Titanic's* sinking in journals such as the *New York Times*, the *Scientific American* and *Lloyd's Weekly* identified her as such. At least one former official of Harland and Wolff is on record giving the original name as *Gigantic*. Moreover, the name makes sense. The words "olympic" and "titanic" both signify huge, imposing, grand--in other words, gigantic. The three names are all cut from the same cloth. Following the *Titanic* debacle, of course, bigness *per se* became a liability for the large liners already plying the Atlantic and naming a new ship *Gigantic* would have been tempting fate--particularly for the steamship line that had just suffered the most gigantic maritime disaster in history. So, White Star officials dug into their bag of names and came up with *Britannic*, a name that not only had an honorable history with the company, but had a certain patriotic ring to it (even if the line was American owned!). A booklet issued at the launch (the cover of which is reproduced here and from which the opening chapter quotation was taken) waxed eloquent on the meaning of the new ship:

[The White Star Line] initiated the "Olympic" type of leviathan, thus maintaining their record as pioneers in the most notable triumphs of Naval Architecture and Marine Engineering during the past half-century: i. e., during the most progressive period in the history of the world's commerce, the White Star Line have played an important and conspicuous part in the far-reaching developments fraught with so much benefit to mankind. Ships and shipping are amongst the links that bind not only the British Empire together, but the whole commercial world. Distant parts of the earth are brought nearer, people of different nationalities ever more closely and continuously in touch with each other, the diffusion of knowledge is increased, trade and commerce expands; and if, as has been so well said, "Commerce is the handmaid of Peace," the services of a great organisation like the White Star Line to the cause of international amity are incalculable. This is especially the case in regard to the United Kingdom and the United States of

At the time the Britannic was launched, the booklet, above, was issued. It went into great detail on the mechanical aspects of the new ship, but included almost nothing regarding interior features or decor. The launch date was February 26, 1914.

America; and in the celebration of the hundred years' peace between these two great branches of the Anglo-Saxon race, a handsome tribute might justly be paid to the White Star Line for their share of the beneficent influence exerted by the Shipping Trade towards this happy consummation...In the "Britannic" the White Star Line have, for the second time, espoused a name that appeals to both sides of the Atlantic, where the kinship of blood is cemented by the close ties of mutual interest and manly esteem.

Whew! And, all this time we thought they were peddling boat rides...

The blood and manly esteem of the Anglo-Saxon race aside, the *Britannic* was slated to be the third member of the triad begun by the *Olympic* and *Titanic*, to provide the White Star Line with 46,000 ton weekly departure capabilities from both New York and Southampton. As such, she was intended to be similar the first two. The designs would have been much closer still had it not been for the *Titanic* disaster, an event which forced a major rebuilding of the *Olympic*. Work was suspended on the *Gigantic* and numerous design changes--and name changes!--were made before work was recommenced. The most obvious of these was with regard to the lifeboats, but there were other significant ones, as well.

The alterations in the *Britannic* made her the largest in gross tonnage of the three: at a 48,158 tons, she was about 5% heavier when fitted as a hospital ship and probably would have been about 50,000 tons (about 10% heavier) when fitted as a commercial liner. Most of this added weight was due to increased internal compartmentalization, to the giant-sized lifeboat davits, to somewhat heavier construction throughout and to a whole list of safety gear and redundant systems. Not surprisingly, following the *Titanic* debacle the White Star Line was obsessed with safety.

Reinforced bulkheads and plating were used from the tank top right up through F Deck and the watertight bulkheads extended up to the Bridge Deck. The *Titanic* had been designed to remain afloat with any two compartments flooded. The *Britannic* was designed to

Right, two photographs of the Britannic under construction. She was built in the Olympic's old slip in the Great Gantry at Harland and Wolff, above. She appears almost ready for the launch at this point. Below, the launch photographed from the harbor.

survive flooding in any six.

The lifeboat davits on the *Britannic* were at once the most unsightly and most ingenious ever engineered for a liner--but, of course, this was now a particular sore point with the White Star Line. As was the case with most major equipment, they were Harland and Wolff's own design. They could service not one or two lifeboats at each station, but six. White Star claimed that they could lower the boats from the next station over, as well, i. e., a starboard davit could reach over and lower the six boats (one at a time) from the port lifeboat station directly opposite. Thus, no matter what the list, all boats could be lowered from the safest, most feasible side of the ship. If the davits were actually able to do all that, their arrangement on the ship was bizarre. Of the five davits fitted along the Boat Deck (three on the starboard side, two on the port side), three of them were placed abreast of funnels, making any reaching to the other side a patent impossibility.

Accommodations were projected for 2,500 passengers and 950 crew. The facilities in the *Olympic* and *Titanic* were improved upon, particularly in first class with more private baths and the addition of a fourth elevator. Artist renderings of the proposed interiors show them to have been a bit more ornate than those on her sisters. The Promenade Deck, which was entirely open on the *Olympic*, was enclosed for about one-third of its length on both the *Titanic* and the *Britannic*. In addition, the Well Deck on the *Britannic* was also enclosed.

On July 2, 1914, it was announced by the company that the *Britannic* would commence service between Southampton and New York in the spring of 1915. The war, however, intervened and the unfinished ship remained in Belfast. She was essentially completed except for her interior fittings and decor. After the war, these were auctioned off and reportedly included, among other materials, 120,000 square feet of wood paneling (70,000 feet of mahogany and 50,000 feet of oak).

The *Britannic* was requisitioned by the Admiralty on November 13, 1915, and officially completed as a hospital ship by December 12th. While on a trip from Salonika on November 21, 1916, she was sunk in the Kea Channel in the Aegean. The explosion took place on the starboard side shortly after 8 a.m. and she went down in about 55 minutes. The explosion apparently occurred at the watertight bulkhead between holds #2 and #3. The bulkhead separating holds #2 and #1 was also damaged. At the same time, boiler rooms #5 and #6 began taking water. Thus, the area of damage was roughly the same as that sustained by the *Titanic* four-and-a-half years earlier.

The magnitude of the damage was revealed by Jacques Cousteau in an expedition in 1976. The ship is lying on her starboard side in about 375 feet of water and, for all practical purposes, her bow is blown away forward of hold #3. Her hull below the Shelter Deck is completely gone at the bulkhead separating holds #2 and #3. The hull and sections of the keel simply aren't there for a distance of perhaps 60-70 feet! The bow section remains attached to the rest of the ship primarily by the upper decks. The port side hull plates are bent outward, indicating a tremendous explosion from inside the ship. The best guess is that the mine or torpedo struck her in her reserve coal locker igniting the coal dust.

The captain, Charles Bartlett, stayed at his post until all on board had been sent away in the 35 lifeboats lowered. Rescue vessels were on the scene in several hours. Of more than 1,100 on board, only 30 died. Another 45 were wounded. Most of the deaths reportedly occurred as the ship remained underway when two port lifeboats were launched prematurely and were sucked into the still turning screws. As a strange

Above, an artist's rendering of the first class grand stairway on the Britannic (Harland and Wolff photo, courtesy Gary R. Spence). The interiors designed for the Britannic were, in general, somewhat more ornate than those on the Olympic and Titanic. Little of the interior decor was ever installed, though, and most was put up for auction after the war. A major feature of the Britannic was her out-sized lifeboat davits, below as shown in the launch booklet. They could handle six boats each.

HARLAND & WOLFF'S PATENT BOAT-LOWERING GEAR.

DAVITS INBOARD.

DAVITS IN OUTBOARD POSITION WITH BOAT SUSPENDED.

footnote to the tragedy, one of the crew members, Violet Jessup, had been a member of the crew on the *Titanic*! She survived both sinkings.

There was considerable controversy over whether the *Britannic* had been sunk by a mine or by a torpedo. The channel had supposedly been cleared of mines the day before and there were reports of submarine sightings in the area. Still, the naval board of inquiry was unable to reach a conclusion either way. It all seems rather academic in retrospect and the best evidence is that it was a mine, but a torpedo would have pleased many. Torpedoing a hospital ship would have been yet another example of the wickedness of the Hun and one more propaganda tool for the British cause.

The *Britannic* was the largest single loss in the British Merchant Marine during the war and a tremendous blow to the White Star Line. Added to the demise of the *Titanic*, it was a combination of calamities from which the line never fully recovered.

Right, two views of the Britannic. She was intended as a passenger liner, above as depicted in this rare White Star card, and had she been completed as one would have looked very much like her two sisters. Of course, by the time the Britannic was launched, the Titanic was long gone and the loss of that ship, the second of the three, had a profound effect on the other two. The Olympic was extensively rebuilt and the Britannic, on the stocks at Harland and Wolff at that time, underwent numerous design--and name--changes. (She had begun life as the Gigantic.) The Britannic, had she been completed as a liner, would have most closely resembled the Titanic for, like the Titanic, her Promenade Deck was partially enclosed. The Britannic's main identifying feature, however, was her giant lifeboat davits. Those on the Titanic were fitted with one lifeboat each. Those on the Britannic were designed to handle as many as six. Understandably, the White Star Line was obsessed with lifeboats at this point. The Britannic was also extensively subdivided in such a way that her watertight compartments could withstand the sort of calamity that befell the Titanic. If ever there should have been an unsinkable ship, this should have been it. When she went into service as a hospital ship during World War I, however, she struck a mine in the Aegean and sank in only 55 minutes--almost 2 hours faster than the Titanic. Underwater exploration has since revealed that the mine apparently touched off a massive coal dust explosion in one of the forward bunkers all but blowing away the forward part of the ship.

Chapter 9.
Titanic's Lucky
Sister Part II:
Olympic, 1913-37

The *Olympic* is chosen by travelers who respond to the appeal of real dignity and quiet elegance. These people board the *Olympic* with that air of assurance which distinguishes people whose choice is unfailingly correct. (From a 1920s White Star Line brochure)

The only one of the three great White Star sister ships to complete a peacetime voyage, the *Olympic*

survived some difficult early experiences to become the Grand Old Lady of the North Atlantic, plying the sea lanes for nearly a quarter-of-a-century. When completed, she was the largest liner in world. She lost that honor for the few days the *Titanic* was in service, then regained it until the German *Imperator* (later the Cunard *Berengaria*) was completed in 1913. She remained the largest British-built liner until the *Queen Mary*.

The pre-*Titanic* career of the *Olympic* was told in Chapter 4. The *Olympic* was in mid-Atlantic when the *Titanic* met her doom, but too far away to do more than lend her powerful Marconi radio capabilities for the transmission of messages. As the sister ship, however, the *Olympic* could hardly have hoped to avoid some repercussions. The first indication of this came upon her arrival in England following the tragedy. Balking crew members refused to board her until she was equipped with sufficient life-saving capacity for all the passengers and crew. Since lifeboats could not be installed with

adequate haste, the ship was littered with life rafts for that voyage and the five remaining voyages of the 1912 season. The *Olympic* was then retired temporarily from service and returned to Harland and Wolff for extensive rebuilding. It didn't really matter much, as customers avoided the ship in droves. Those same travelers who, only a few weeks earlier, thought the bigger the safer, now avoided big ships of all lines on general principle.

The sinking of the *Titanic* had been a severe blow to the entire British shipping industry, but the White Star Line and Harland and Wolff were determined to restore public confidence in the *Olympic*. To do this, they knew that they had to address the very real design shortcomings that had been so well publicized in the hearings that looked into the sinking of the *Titanic*.

The *Olympic* spent six months back at Harland and Wolff in the winter of 1912-13 being extensively rebuilt at a cost of $1,215,000. The double bottom was extended up the sides to a point above the water line, forming a double skin. This was not minor surgery, needless to say, and, according to reports required the removal of funnels and boilers, replacement of the piping and a good deal of the wiring.

In addition to the above, the obvious alteration--a dramatic increase in lifeboat capacity--was carried out, too. Following the rebuilding, lifeboats lined the boat deck on both sides, sometimes "nested," or stacked in twos. As a result of all the changes, the *Olympic* that emerged for the 1913 season was undoubtedly one of the safest ships ever to sail the seas. She was also slightly larger in tonnage, with an increase to 46,350 tons being recorded. Despite this, first class accommodations were somewhat reduced.

The *Olympic* returned to service paired with the *Majestic* (1889) and *Oceanic* (1899), both aging and hardly of the same caliber. The White Star Line, however, had little choice. The *Olympic* quickly regained its popularity in the months leading up to the outbreak of war and, in fact, many sailed on her precisely because she was the sister of the celebrated *Titanic*. (There a was sort of *Titanic* chic developing for a while.) In time, though, the *Olympic* became one of the most popular of the North Atlantic liners for her own exceptional qualities.

Above, the Olympic looked especially imposing in the floating dry-dock at Southampton. The liner had to be raised 40 feet out of the water by the dry-dock, which was quite a task, considering that 46,000 tons were involved. The process took nearly four hours.

Along with just about everything else, advertising styles changed during the two-and-a-half decades the Olympic was in service. Compare the delicate Art Deco magazine ad from 1933, above, to the ornate cover of the 1912 post-Titanic Olympic brochure below.

The outbreak of war on August 4, 1914, found the *Olympic* on her way to New York. She completed that voyage, then switched from Southampton to Glasgow for the British terminus and continued commercial voyages for several months. As there was very little eastbound traffic, much of this time was spent ferrying an estimated 6,000 American nationals from the war zone back to New York. It was on one of these voyages that the first of her war adventures occurred.

Passing Lough Swilly off the coast of Ireland, the *Olympic* happened upon the British battleship *Audacious* just after the latter had struck a mine. The *Audacious* was a new ship of the King George V Class and displaced 23,000 tons, making her about half the size of the *Olympic*. The *Olympic* stopped to render assistance, a humanitarian action that, in retrospect, was probably rather stupid. Her master not only risked brushing into any one of the unknown number of mines in the area, but, for the duration of the rescue, she was a sitting duck for any passing German submarine--and a fabulous prize at that. Her luck held, though, which is more than could be said for the unfortunate battleship. The *Olympic* took off most of the warship's crew then attempted to take her in tow. Due to heavy seas, however, the tow was unsuccessful and the *Audacious* sank. The Admiralty imposed a news blackout on the whole incident and even went so far as to confiscate film from passengers on the *Olympic*! The more things change, the more they remain the same...

The *Olympic* was commissioned as a naval transport in September, 1915. In this guise, she made four trips to the Mediterranean in connection with the Dardanelles and Gallipoli campaigns. Late in the year, she was attacked by an enemy submarine but was able to use a combination of speed and evasive maneuvers to escape unharmed.

In February, 1916, the *Olympic* was attacked twice again by enemy submarines and twice again emerged unscathed. The *Britannic* was not so lucky. She was sunk in the Aegean the same year, reportedly by a mine, although some said it was a torpedo. At that bitter moment, the *Olympic* became the sole survivor among the fabulous Olympic Class liners: the *Olympic*, the *Titanic* and the *Gigantic/Britannic*.

In March, 1916, she was returned temporarily to the White Star Line. During this period, she was fitted with six 6-inch guns for submarine defense. In April, 1916, the *Olympic* was chosen to host an important British diplomatic mission to the United States. The delegation, headed by A. J. Balfour, was delivered to

R.M.S. "OLYMPIC," 46,359
(The largest British Steame

Viewed from a Seaplane while on War

The Olympic had a busy and exciting career during World War I. She transported a grand total of 119,000 civilians and troops, steamed 184,000 miles and burned 347,000 tons of coal. In the process, she survived four known attacks by enemy submarines. To help ward off submarine attacks, she was "dazzle" painted with wild colors and geometric shapes (see above).

Halifax, Nova Scotia, in Canada, then returned from the United States to Britain.

For the rest of the war, the *Olympic* was engaged in trooping duties, bringing American and Canadian fighting men to the war front. For this service, she was "dazzle" painted (see the illustration in this chapter). Dazzle painting was a fairly bizarre tactic used to ward off submarine attacks by (hopefully) rendering ships optically untrackable. That was the theory, at least. It is not recorded whether it worked against competent submariners--and the tactic was not revived by the British during World War II--but while it lasted it certainly made for uniquely colorful ocean travel!

In May, 1918, during its twenty-second trooping voyage, the *Olympic* met her greatest adventure of the war. She was attacked by German submarine U-103. The torpedo was avoided by quick evasive action, but then the *Olympic* did a remarkable thing. She turned on her attacker and rammed it! Actually, the blow to the submarine was described as "glancing," but even a light blow from a 46,000 ton ship is quite a wallop and the submarine immediately began to sink. Some of the German crew managed to escape and were picked-up by a passing American destroyer.

By the end of the war, in November, 1918, the *Olympic* had compiled an impressive record in service to the Allied cause. Without casualty, she had transported 41,000 civilian passengers, 66,000 troops (two-thirds of them American, the rest Canadian), and 12,000 members of a Chinese labor battalion--119,000 people in all. In so doing, she steamed a grand total of 184,000 miles, burned 347,000 tons of coal and survived four known attacks by enemy submarines. She proudly carried the affectionate nickname, "Old Reliable," bestowed upon her by those who sailed her. The curse of the *Titanic* had finally been laid to rest.

During the first part of 1919, the *Olympic* worked hard to repatriate thousands of troops to the New World. That finished, she was returned to Harland and Wolff for a $2,430,000 refurbishing and refitting for postwar commercial service. The key alteration was the conversion from coal to oil burning boilers. This enabled the "black gang" working the boiler rooms to be cut in number from 350 to only 60 men--an 83%

Left, are a couple of the handsome White Star Line cards issued for the Olympic after the war. The one on top is probably late-1920s vintage. The bottom one dates from the 1930s, the last Olympic card ever issued. There was a Cunard imprint revision in 1934-35.

reduction. Coaling in port was always a messy business and coal handling was the dirtiest, most difficult work on board a liner. Add to that the reputation of the black gang, who tended to be a violent and unsavory lot, together with the dislocations caused by the periodic British coal strikes, and the reasons for oil conversion were compelling.

While the *Olympic* was being reworked, the Red Star liner *Lapland* was substituted on the North Atlantic run under White Star colors. The Red Star Line was another member of the IMM group, and the smaller ships were sometimes shifted back and forth. When she returned to service, the *Olympic* was almost like a new ship, having been completely renovated from stem to stern. Her postwar accommodations comprised 750 first class, 500 second class and 1,150 third class passengers. She made her first postwar voyage in July, 1920.

The old *Majestic* and *Oceanic* were memories at this point and the White Star Line badly needed a couple of modern running mates for the *Olympic*. The Cunard Line had a similar problem with the *Mauretania*, which, of course, lost her sister when the *Lusitania* was torpedoed off Ireland in 1915. The United States lost no big liners--having had none to lose--but joined the British in appropriating as war reparations every important German liner in sight.

The *Imperator* went to Cunard. Renamed the *Berengaria*, it joined the *Mauretania* and *Aquitania* on the North Atlantic. The United States Lines got the *Vaterland* even before the end of the war (the Germans had allowed it to be interned in an American port for safe-keeping!) and had it extensively rebuilt. Renamed the *Leviathan*, and dubbed the "Levi Nation" by American dough boys, it did well in trooping duty during the war but never made money in commercial service. It had no suitable running mates and was avoided like the plague even by many American travelers--perhaps especially by American travelers--because it didn't serve liquor. (America was under the puritan grip of Prohibition at this point. Foreign liners locked up their liquor stores while in American ports, but were joyously awash in Demon Rum as soon as the three-mile-limit was reached. The United States Lines, under the thumb of the American government, stayed

The Olympic and her postwar running mates are shown at right. The Olympic is in the middle with her with "nested" lifeboats, circa 1930. The Majestic is shown above. The Homeric appears at the bottom. The Olympic was by far the most successful of the three.

pure--and broke.)

The White Star Line finally got two of the Germans war prizes, the *Columbus*, renamed the *Homeric*, and the unfinished *Bismarck*. This latter ship was, at 56,551 tons, the largest in the world at that time. Launched before the war, but never fitted out, she was completed by Blohm and Voss, the German shipbuilder, to White Star specifications as the third *Majestic*. It was bad enough to have the prides of the German merchant marine stolen away, but to have to build one just to lose it was too much for many Germans. The fitting out process of the *Majestic* was clouded by dark rumors of sabotage and punctuated with threats that the ship would never leave the Fatherland. It all turned out to be talk, though, and the *Majestic* joined the White Star fleet in 1922 without incident.

This new *Majestic* was a fine ship in many respects and featured, among other things, the first sound movie theater afloat as soon as talkies came in. Despite this, British and American travelers always seemed to prefer the traditionally British *Olympic* and the *Homeric* was even less successful. At 34,351 tons, she was substantially smaller than the other two and much slower. She would have been better suited to cruise service, perhaps, but White Star needed her for the North Atlantic Ferry. For what it was worth--which wasn't much--the *Homeric* was the largest vessel in the world equipped with old-fashioned reciprocating engines.

(Of the three big German liners appropriated as war reparations, the *Leviathan*, ironically enough, was the soundest ship. The Americans had completely refurbished her after the war, including rewiring. The *Berengaria* and *Majestic* retained their original, and apparently inferior, German wiring and suffered from chronic electrical problems throughout their years of British service. It was not unusual for them, especially as they got older, to catch fire due to electrical shorts. As a consequence, many voyages were made with crew members engaged around the clock fighting smoldering mini-infernoes hidden behind panelling or buried in any of the hundreds of dark recesses scattered throughout the ships. Eventually, the *Berengaria* was officially declared a fire hazard by New York fire inspectors, an event which spelled an ignominious end to her career. The

Three views of the Olympic in the early 1920s appear here. The photo, facing page, was taken from a photo card actually mailed from the ship in 1925. The other two cards are contemporary artist's renditions of the ship--with a lot of artistic license in evidence.

Majestic never suffered that fate. It is interesting to note, though, that, in 1939, after being sold to the British navy and refitted as a cadet training ship, she caught fire and was destroyed.)

Throughout the twenties, there was periodic talk of a new running mate for the *Olympic*, but nothing ever seemed to come of it. In the meantime, the *Olympic* continued to go about her business in fine style and continuing popularity, especially with the "old" money that regularly sailed the Atlantic.

In 1924, while leaving New York, the *Olympic* suffered her third collision since being launched. This time it was with the Furness liner, *Ford Hamilton* (formerly the *Bermudan*). It wasn't much of a collision, however, as such things go. There were no casualties and both ships made it into port under their own power.

In 1927, IMM sold White Star to the Royal Mail Line group. The main benefit of this sale was that it placed the White Star Line back under British control, something apparently deemed worth the expense by shipping interests in Britain, who were still smarting over the American take-over at the turn of the century.

The Americans were not out of the picture completely, though--at least indirectly. In, 1923, the United States Congress had passed a law drastically revising the immigration regulations. The prime result, insofar as the transatlantic steamship companies were concerned, was to make it much more difficult to attract third class passengers. All the big liners were affected by this, the *Olympic* included, and the whole thrust of the trade was irrevocably altered as a result. In the late-twenties, the *Olympic* was modernized, in large part to reflect these changed realities in the marketplace. Passenger accommodations were changed to 675 first class, 560 "tourist" (formerly "second") class and 830 third class. Later, accommodations were revised again to create 618 first class, 447 tourist class and a mere 380 third class passengers. The simple truth was that the numbers of passengers sailing the Atlantic were being sharply reduced and the various steamship lines were each dealing with that fact as best they could.

In 1929, a new 60,000 ton companion for the *Olympic* was finally laid down at Harland and Wolff. Many knowledgeable observers in the shipping trade predicted that White Star would never find the money to build such a ship--and, sure enough, they didn't. Nostalgically named the *Oceanic*, only the keel was ever completed due to the tightening financial condition of the company. Two much smaller motor ships were, however, finished: the *Georgic* and *Britannic*. They were the last ships ever delivered to the White Star Line.

In 1933-34, the *Olympic* was sent back to Belfast for extensive engine work. She was replaced temporarily on the North Atlantic by the *Georgic*. The year 1934 also saw a couple of fateful events for the *Olympic*. The first was the merger of the White Star and Cunard companies. This was done under heavy pressure from the British government and White Star was definitely the junior partner in the new Cunard White Star company. All Cunard and White Star ships continued to wear their traditional colors, but all new ships were painted as Cunarders and most of the fine old White Star ships were soon sold or scrapped.

In May, 1934, the second fateful event occurred, this one involving serious loss of life. The *Olympic*, steaming in a fog, rammed and sank the famous Nantucket Light Ship, seven of whose crew members were lost. The *Olympic* was held solely to blame and the line was ordered to pay $500,000 in compensation.

In March, 1935, the *Olympic* was laid up at Southampton. In August, she was opened for public inspection with the idea of finding a buyer. In September, she was purchased for $500,000 by a British industrialist and then resold to the ship-breaking firm of Thomas Ward on the condition that she be sent to their Jarrow, Scotland, yard for scrapping. The idea was to provide work for Scottish laborers suffering under the weight of the Depression. The *Olympic* left Southampton for the final time on October 11, 1935. She was stripped down to her hull by August, 1936, and scrapped completely by September, 1937.

These unusual photos were used by White Star for publicity purposes in the mid-1920s. The remarkable photo on the facing page was taken from the top of the fourth funnel looking forward and revealing a hazy view of Manhattan ahead with the White Star pier being dwarfed on the right. The fourth funnel was a dummy on both the Olympic and Titanic. It was basically there for show, but there was a hard commercial purpose behind it, too. The immigrant trade was vitally important to the steamship companies and many would-be immigrant customers, it was said, judged a ship by its funnels. A two funnel ship was likely to be bigger and faster--and therefore better--than a one funnel ship. Three funnels were better than two, four better than three, five...oops! On this page, the photo was probably taken from the roof of the pier, judging from the angle. It affords an excellent view of the arrangement of the lifeboats and rafts along the Boat Deck.

Acknowledgments

It is a curious thing with books. Speaking solely from the author's point of view, I willingly confess that any worthwhile book is the product, directly or indirectly, of the work of many. Yet, the author gets all the credit. Life, as John F. Kennedy was wont to observe, is unfair. (Of course, the publishers and distributors get all the money, but that's another subject entirely!)

I would be remiss if I failed to express my thanks to several people who have helped me with my collection over the years and with assembling material specifically for this volume. Carl House, one of America's premier steamship archivists, has lent invaluable support, to say nothing of several of the illustrations that appear on these pages. Robert Mason, one of Britain's premier steamship archivists, has likewise been a font of seemingly unending encouragement and assistance. And, if I may get maudlin for a moment (but, I promise, only for a moment) their friendship has been one of the true joys of being involved in the steamship field.

Gary R. Spence, a *Titanic* authority of the first water, was enormously helpful in numerous ways. He protected me from a couple of major embarrassments by proofing the manuscript for factual and technical errors. He also lent a number of items from his personal collection that made a real difference in the book, including a couple of the illustrations that appear on these pages. The ultimate accuracy of this book owes a lot to his efforts, although he is absolved of any responsibility for whatever errors may remain.

In addition, Richard Faber, one of this country's leading dealers in steamship memorabilia, has shown, at critical junctures, a truly remarkable ability to locate just those items I have needed to build my archives. I should also thank my mother, for it was she who got me started on this subject some 30 years ago with the gift of a copy of Walter Lord's magnum opus, *A Night to Remember*. Finally, I owe a debt of gratitude to my editor, Ed Lehwald. He has, as always, managed to save me from my worst stylistic excesses and, in general, done everything a first class editor is supposed to do.

It can honestly be said that without the support of these six, this book would not have been published. Thank you, one and all.

The usual final comment: I have endeavored to make this book as balanced and accurate as possible. I would like to hear of any errors so that future editions may be brought up to date. Write to me in care of the address for Bookman Publishing listed in the front of the book. I would also like to hear from anyone who may have archival material that might assist my on-going research.

Index